HOW *I* PLANNED *Your* WEDDING

The All-True Story of a Mother and Daughter Surviving the Happiest Day of Their Lives

SUSAN WIGGS
ELIZABETH WIGGS MAAS

HARLEQUIN®

HOW I PLANNED *Your* WEDDING

ISBN-13: 978-0-373-89227-3

www.eHarlequin.com

Printed in U.S.A.

We dedicate this book to each other.
It's a tribute to our mother-daughter bond, to the love
and trust we share, and a celebration of our epic
sixteen months of struggle and triumph.

Contents

ONCE UPON A TIME... THE JOURNEY BEGINS

ELIZABETH

I was born to be a bride. There are family photographs of me in a bridal gown dating all the way back to age two. Even in my imagination, every detail was precisely arranged—the flowers, the veil, the tiara, the sparkly shoes, the smear of lipstick across my mouth. But in those little-girl fantasies, there was one small missing detail: the groom.

Then, senior year of college, the heavens opened up, angels sang from on high and one tipsy night I found myself alone with Dave. I'd seen him around school before (after all, there were only 1,500 students at our tiny liberal arts college), but something about him was... different. Specifically, he looked like a god. Over the summer, he'd grown his glossy, blond hair past his shoulders and had sprouted an extra six inches in height, taking him to a towering 6-foot-4. Pair that with his gracefully lean cross-country runner's body and I'd bagged myself the offspring of Brad Pitt and a Thomson's gazelle.

During that first fateful night in his dorm room when we had, ahem, chastely chatted from opposite ends of the futon, he asked if I wanted to brush my teeth, to which I replied "Hell, yes" because, you know, stale cheap beer breath isn't the most romantic thing in the world. As soon as our pearly whites were clean and fresh, Dave looked at me and began slowly leaning in, a gentlemanly question in his eyes, waiting for my signal that, yes, he could now storm the citadel on his steed, breaching the gates of my...well, you know. I'm not one for sub-tlety, so I grabbed him by the ears and yanked him into the make-out session to end all make-out sessions. And that's about all I'm going to say about *that*, Dear Readers. I'm collaborating with my *mother* on this project, after all.

As it turns out, that was the *last* "first" kiss I would ever share with a man, though I didn't know it at the time. I certainly hoped so, because it was *that* magical, the kiss that erased all others. The defin-ing smooch. The zing of chemistry between Dave and me was palpable. After growing up under the wing of a bestselling writer, I finally, *finally* understood what my mom's books were really about—and why they're so addictive to so many readers. Dave and I spent countless hours talk-ing and cracking each other up, falling under that magical spell that has launched a million romance novels.

Exactly three years, seven months and twenty-two days later, I would kiss this same dude in a sunlit, fountain-fed atrium full of our family and friends: our first kiss as husband and wife. But between that first Pabst Blue Ribbon–fueled make-out session and the moment we sealed our marriage with a kiss, we had a mountain to climb. A moun-tain of friggin' insane wedding planning that would, no matter how we fought it, be heavily supervised and directed by a woman who creates over-the-top, happily-ever-after romance for a living: my mom.

SUSAN

Of all the dreams I ever dreamed for my daughter, the biggest one was the dream in which she finds the one person in the world who will love her for the rest of her life. Because, after all, love in all its forms gives life its meaning. I've always believed that. I'd *better* believe that. I've made a career out of it, after all.

But when it comes to real-world matters, there's a deeper reason for wanting your child to spend the rest of her days with the love of her life. It's the one secret you can't tell her. She has to find out for herself. A lasting love is the deepest of life's joys.

When Elizabeth was very little, and people asked what she wanted to be when she grew up, she didn't say a teacher or a doctor, an artist or a sales clerk or a hot-air balloon pilot.

She would tell them, "A bride."

My friends would offer pitying looks. "I'm so sorry. She'll grow out of it. She'll realize that what she really wants is to be a rocket scientist or a chef or a choreographer..."

I didn't really need their pity, and I wasn't bothered by her oft-stated aspiration. As a romance writer, I never quibbled with her dream. Of course she wanted to be a bride. She wanted to find the man of her dreams and live happily ever after.

Is there any higher calling? Any bigger dream?

And so I let her fantasy grow and develop, unimpeded by other people's expectations or even common sense. The vision was embellished with horse-drawn carriages made of crystal, a banquet consisting of nothing but French toast, Skittles and spun sugar, a ball gown so elaborate it wouldn't even fit through doorways. The bride would be attended by her best and most beautiful friends, including her Airedale terrier.

When it came time to plan her actual wedding, this vision stayed more or less intact. Sure, the horse-drawn carriage morphed into a white stretch limo, complete with glittering disco lights in the ceiling, and the family dog had gone over the rainbow bridge, but overall, her dream came true—the gown, the beautiful friends, the hair, the pearls...

But where does that leave me, the mom?

I'm not quite sure how to say this, so I'll be blunt. Does anybody actually dream about being the *mother* of the bride?

Come on. That's kind of like getting stuck with Midge—the sidekick—while playing Barbies. It's also sure to mess with your denial about exactly how old you are.

Hello? You are now old enough to actually have a daughter who's getting married. A new generation has come along, and here you thought *you* were the young generation. You didn't even notice the runner behind you, reaching forward to pass you the baton.

Deal with it. No, do better than that. Embrace it. And don't forget to savor the process. After all, that's what you've been doing all her life, I suspect.

If you're like me, the mother of an adored and indulged child who has owned your heart for the past twentysomething years, you remember every single minute. You remember what her toddler voice sounded like when she laughed. You remember the little-girl smell of her, and dresses that were too expensive but you bought them anyway because you just had to see her in that adorable smocked pinafore. You remember the feel of her tiny—usually sticky—hand in yours as you took her into unfamiliar situations: A swimming pool. Kindergarten. The IMAX. A petting zoo. Her first piano recital. The dentist. You remember the victory dance she did to celebrate accomplishments from winning a race in a swim meet to learning cursive writing in the third grade. You remember laughing so hard your sides ached, and holding her when she cried, willing to trade your soul to keep her from hurting. You remember how much she loved goodnight kisses, how much she hated black olives, and how very sure she was that you would always be the center of her world.

And then, before you know it, this poised and accomplished young woman appears—seemingly out of nowhere—with a young man at her side. And not just any young man. *The* young man. Prince Charming. The forever guy.

They have Big News. They can't wait to tell you. Turns out Prince Charming has even been conspiring with your husband, arranging the surprise proposal, the whirlwind romantic weekend, the start of plans that are about to consume you for the next sixteen months.

All right, so you're not the center of her world anymore. You're the Mother of the Bride. Even the phrase itself makes you sound old. Dowdy.

But here's a secret: you're in for the time of your life.

1

ENGAGEMENT

In which Prince Charming
proposes to ~~us~~, er, me

ELIZABETH

EARLY MARCH

"So, my publisher just called and asked if there are any dates this summer when I won't be able to go on a book tour," said my mom.

I have this habit—which I believe is absolutely adorable and endearing—of calling my mother every time I'm walking anywhere. The result is that we speak at least four or five times a day, and she's gotten into the habit of answering phone calls from me with, "Where are you walking?" This particular conversation happened one morning as I hiked the five blocks between my bus stop and work.

My mom got a weird tone in her voice and continued. "And...I'm just telling yoo-oooou about my summer planssss..." (in a singsong voice) "...because I was wondering if there might be any sort of, you know, *event* around that time. You know, like a family event here in Seattle that I will have to attend because it will be a *very big deal for our family?*"

"Er..."

"Your wedding, Elizabeth."

Right. There was just one problem. One of the parties involved—namely, Dave—was not exactly down with the whole wedding thing. Oh, I'm pretty sure he had plenty of hopes, dreams, expectations, maybe even obsessions about building a future with me. But, like most guys, he played his cards close to the vest and he wasn't fond of showing his hand. Not even to me, the love of his life.

This was starting to grate on my mother. She held her tongue and cultivated patience, and I did my best to follow her example.

But okay, I'll just say it. Listen up, ladies. When it's time, it's time.

The man of your dreams gets a grace period, but by definition, a grace period has an end point. Dave's was quickly approaching.

After reassuring my mother that, indeed, she would be the first person to know upon my engagement to Dave, my Canadian boyfriend whom I met in college, I changed the subject so that we wouldn't jinx anything. I understood her concern. Dave and I had recently decided to move to Chicago for him to attend law school. As usual, I didn't really have a plan for myself beyond being blond, watching every riveting moment of *The View* and waiting for my dream job to fall into my lap.

Unlike the fictional gals in my mom's books, I was not a spunky-yet-lovable virgin trying to save the family ranch in the face of staggering adversity, all the while raising her dead sister's children and dallying with some tattooed bad boy named Rusty or Ryder.

I was a real, actual person. Maybe a lot like you—just out of school, crazy in love, trying to make sense out of my life.

So, yeah, I was also wondering if this new level of commitment— namely, picking up and moving to the Windy City—would result in an engagement. (Spoiler: It did.)

Later that evening, Dave and I walked home hand-in-hand. I was a bit tipsy because we had joined friends for happy hour and I gracelessly steered our conversation to the upcoming wedding of two of our closest friends. HINT, HINT, Dave. When he acted clueless, I brought up the conversation I'd had with my mom about her summer plans.

"You know," I slurred, "my mom was asking when we were going to get engaged...ha ha, isn't that HILARIOUS?"

Dave shot me a sidelong glance and said, "Don't talk to her about it so much. I want it to be natural, not something that our families push us into doing."

See, here's the cute thing about Dave. As the middle son of three boys, he doesn't have a clue about the mother-daughter bond. He doesn't understand that my mother has been party to every single detail of our relationship since before we even began dating. In fact, she was the one who logged into my Facebook account senior year of college, spotted his devastatingly handsome profile picture, and "poked" him on my behalf.

This is the kind of thing that lends credence to the old adage, "Mother Knows Best." Because that poke led to a silly online flirtation, which led to a silly in-person flirtation, which led to me finding my soul's puzzle piece in the form of a 6-foot-4 Canadian runner with a mane of shoulder-length, blond hair. Frickin' awesome. Cue the make-out session I mentioned earlier. My mom couldn't write it better in one of her books. And the Davester had no idea it all started with a click of my mom's mouse.

So when Dave asked me to avoid talking to my mom about the prospect of a proposal, I nodded and kept my mouth shut. The poor guy didn't have a clue. My mother had been the puppet-master of our relationship since before he even knew I existed. I just counted us lucky that we actually did find true love with one another in spite—or perhaps *because*—of my mother's meddling.

Here's a hint about your mom—the older you get, the smarter she seems.

MARCH 14

"What do you want for your birthday, honey?"

Another conversation with my mom, this one on the way home from work nine days before my twenty-fourth birthday. Please note that there is nothing special about this day. It's not the Ides of March. Valentine's Day is long past. St. Paddy's Day, Easter, Arbor Day, Cinco de Mayo, Talk Like a Pirate Day...none of these most sacred feasts falls on March 14. It's the most random of days. The sort of day from which you expect nothing but the usual ambulatory phone call with your mother.

"Well, I feel like it's bad luck to say this..." I began, "but all I really want is for Dave to propose to me. I can't stop thinking about it!"

A string of promising holidays had come and gone, leaving me deflated. I had no doubt that he loved me, but he didn't seem to be in a hurry to take the next obvious step.

I had secretly begged Santa for a ring, but clearly, he didn't get the memo. Then I thought maybe New Year's Eve would be The Moment. Lots of couples got engaged on New Year's Eve, right? But no, all I got on New Year's was a hoarse voice from karaoke performances of "Super Freak," and a raunchy hangover. Then came Valentine's Day, the ultimate date with destiny. Half the married people I know got engaged on Valentine's Day. But when February 14 rolled around, Dave wrote me a beautiful, loving letter and bought me a giant steak. There was no diamond buried in the meat, though. Undaunted, I studied the calendar for the Next Big Special Day. I have a March birthday, so that was a possibility, but I figured I would *know* if Dave was thinking about proposing, and a little voice in my head told me that he would be waiting until we were settled into our new home in Chicago the following year.

My mom, clearly, shared my view.

I could hear her snort on the phone. "He's not going to propose for your birthday," she said in her most matter-of-fact, I-know-everything voice. "*Trust* me. I would know. Your father is incapable of keeping a secret from me, and he hasn't said a word about a proposal."

"But...maybe Dave's just being really secretive...?"

"Nope. Sorry, hon. He's a guy. That means he's about as secretive as a Golden Retriever with a new tennis ball. We'll just have to work on him this summer." With that statement, she embarked on one of her classic Susan Wiggs–style lectures outlining all the ways we would subtly guide the unsuspecting Dave into asking me to marry him.

In her books, the desperately-in-love heroine triggers a proposal by having her stern-yet-loving dad hold a gun to the hero's head, or by staging a life-threatening fall from a castle tower in a hail of crossbow bolts, or by loudly pondering the virtues of joining a nunnery. I wasn't quite that desperate yet. But I was starting to feel the urge to give him a shove in the right direction. As an inventor of romance and love, my mother was the right person to ask for some hints about delivering my subtle PUH-LEEEEEEEEEEZE ASK ME TO MARRY YOU message.

One thing this process probably did have in common with my mom's fiction—I discovered that the deepest rewards were always found at the most unexpected moments. She was probably right. On my birthday in two weeks, I wasn't going to be getting a ring...it was just too obvious.

At this point, I was approaching our apartment building. I pulled out my key to unlock the front door and noticed a tiny red heart sticker just above the lock. Not thinking much of it, I entered the front hall and, still listening to my mom's ideas on wringing a proposal out of Dave, reached for the handle of the door that led to my hall.

There was another heart sticker just above the knob. "Aw, someone must be having an anniversary," I thought.

"...then we'll get your dad to take Dave golfing and talk to him about how he proposed to me, and there might be some kind of ominous mishap involving a fairway wood and Dave's thick head. And if that doesn't work, I'll 'accidentally' send him an email about a Seattle-area wedding photographer, and then you'll start whispering things about diamond rings to him while he's sleeping each night..." my mom continued, spinning plans as elaborate as the plot of a romance novel.

I turned the corner and saw the front door to my apartment. Dave had told me he would be working late, so I wasn't surprised to find it still locked.

But then I saw yet another little red heart sticker above the knob.

"Uh...Mommy?" (Bear with me; I still call her "Mommy") I said as I unlocked the door. I felt a whooshing sensation in my stomach.

"...do you think I should email his mother? I'm sure she wants you guys to get engaged, too. I can't wait to shop for a mother-of-the-bride dress..."

I opened my door. In front of me, every visible surface was covered with flowers. The floor was carpeted in a thick layer of rose petals, tulips drooped from the walls (I later learned that these were held up by the manliest of substances: duct tape), and bright bouquets bloomed from every table in our living room. Crepe paper streamers swagged the perimeter of the room and "Everything" by Michael Bublé, our song, played softly on our stereo.

Standing in the center of it all was Dave, looking more nervous and happy than I had ever seen him.

My mother was still talking: "...you know, your father and I love Dave like a son, so maybe I could just be frank with him and tell him that it's time to seal the deal..."

"Mommy? MOMMY. I have to go. I have to go!"

"What's wrong? Did your washing machine overflow?" I could hear her launch into a litany of tips on cleaning up soapsuds as I hung up on her.

Half an hour later, I was perched on Dave's lap, staring dewy-eyed at the beautiful emerald-cut solitaire he had given me when he asked me, on bended knee, to be his wife.

"I can't wait to tell my mom!" I gushed. "She and I were just talking about how we didn't think you'd propose anytime soon!"

"Actually, I was thinking that we could wait until tomorrow to start telling people," Dave said. "I want tonight just for us, so we can enjoy the moment."

Yeah, my mom was gonna love that idea.

Thus began my sixteen-month wedding planning journey, an experience that would be defined by my constant attempt to balance my own desires with those of my future husband...and my romance-writing mother. Looking back, the experience was pretty awesome in general, but I'm not going to sugarcoat the fact that there were a few moments of eating-icing-straight-from-the-can stress and Lizzie-Borden-took-an-axe rage.

So this book is my gift to you, who (I'm assuming) are about to embark on a wedding-planning journey of your own. I'm not going to give you any itemized checklists or detailed instructions. I'll leave that to the experts. I'm just going to share my own story with you—the story of a real gal planning a real wedding with a real budget. I didn't have peacocks flown in from Spain for some million-dollar reception and I also didn't hand-make two hundred candles for my guests to take home with them after pulling off a magical wedding for five bucks.

What I did was end up happily ever after with the man of my dreams. I won't tell you it's easy. Nothing worth having ever is.

My mom and I have a mostly normal mother-daughter relationship. There were times that we fought like wet cats over the wedding, and other moments when I looked into her eyes and could see how proud she was of me for becoming the woman I am.

Of course, in the first half hour of being engaged, visions of wet cats hadn't even occurred to me yet. Sitting there with my newly minted fiancé, telling him how important it was for me to share our news with my mom immediately, I had this mental image of my mother's eyes filling with tears as I put on my perfect, white wedding gown for the first time, of her nodding enthusiastically as she crammed her mouth full of lemon-raspberry cake at our menu tasting, of her excitedly begging me to let her throw me four—no, five!—bridal showers.

So, looking into my glowingly happy face, Dave agreed to allow me one teeny, tiny phone call...to my mother.

SUSAN

If you were to look up the phrase *mixed feelings* in the dictionary, I suspect you would find a picture of a newly engaged girl's mother. Of course you want your daughter to find someone to love and cherish her, to build a life and a family with her. But the quest for this elusive person is all very theoretical. Her first love was a squishy doll named

"Baby Bobby," which set the bar pretty low. The idea, we hoped, was that she would trade up.

We used to give nicknames to Elizabeth's boyfriends. A few I recall are "The Lump," "The Bottomless Pit" and "The Project." Some had acronyms: "LAMB" (Little Angry Man Boy) and the unfortunate but accurate "GOAH" (Gayest of All Homosexuals). So as you can imagine, her dad and I had developed a healthy skepticism about her dating choices.

During her senior year of college, she experienced the ubiquitous "Turkey Dump" when a guy known as "The Cipher," who was supposed to come home to meet us at Thanksgiving, bailed on her. Hiding a big maternal sigh of relief, I uttered all the soothing mom clichés: "There are plenty of other fish in the sea," "You need a man like a fish needs a bicycle" and "We'll always have chocolate."

We both agreed that nothing soothes a woman scorned quite like shopping. And thanks to the insane innovation of Facebook, you can shop online for your next boyfriend. She gave me a guided tour of the guys on her college network who had a crush on her. (Note to girls: Until you've found Mr. Right, keep your options open.) Initially, I was not encouraged. There were guys with shirts peeled off, guzzling Jägermeister; guys making Zoolander faces, guzzling Jägermeister; guys giving me the thumbs-up sign, guzzling Jägermeister; guys krumping and guzzling Jägermeister...you get the picture. You've *seen* those pictures. Is guzzling Jägermeister today's prerequisite to romance? Did Mr. Right exist only in my feverish writer's imagination?

And then...cue host-of-angels music...she clicked on a picture of Dave. A young, long-haired matinee idol with good grades, good biceps and boyfriend credentials so stellar I was sure he must be hiding something. After all, the guys I write about are *made up*. "They don't exist," I tell my readers.

She brought him home at Christmas. He was even better in person—confident, charming, humble, tender, honest, funny and completely smitten with the work-in-progress that is my daughter. "He's

SHARING YOUR BIG NEWS WITH THE WORLD

Dave is an intensely private person (which is why the powers that be have challenged him with a loud-mouthed oversharer of a wife), but he knew that we would have to share the news of our engagement—gushy details and all—with a whole mess of people.

The weekend he proposed, he scheduled a studio session with a photographer to capture the first blush of our engaged bliss. The engagement portrait is a relatively new phenomenon and from the outside it sometimes seems like an extension of the Hallmarketization of the wedding industry. I mean, really, what couple needs extra professional photos when they're in the middle of planning what will be the most photographed day of their lives?

However, in my humble opinion, engagement portraits serve an important purpose. Picture your home. Now picture your walls papered with photos of you in a giant white dress. Now imagine that those are the only nice photos that exist of you and your honey.

It's nice and all, but, wouldn't you like to have at least a handful of gorgeous photos with you and your partner looking a little less...bridal? As beautiful as you're going to look on your wedding day, the inherently costumey nature of weddings isn't the easiest thing to base an interior design scheme on. I don't know about you, but I sure as heck don't want to feel like I live inside an issue of *Modern Bride*.

There are other benefits to an engagement photo session, too. Those images will come in handy when you want to announce your engagement in your local newspapers, or when you're designing your wedding website, or putting together your save-the-dates. And it's also a great way to get to know your photographer so that you can feel completely comfortable around him or her on the day of your wedding.

Then, again, maybe you don't like displaying photos of yourself around your house. In which case, skip the engagement portrait. Skip anything you damn well please. This is your wedding.

too good to be true," I told her. "He's not a Project."

"I traded up," she said.

The only nickname we could pin on this guy was "Canadian Dave."

Their courtship was a romantic roller-coaster ride that culminated in the aforementioned proposal. He called my husband to ask for her hand. I later learned he flubbed a key line, telling Jay, "I want to marry your wife. Er, *daughter*. I want to marry your *daughter*."

And lo, it came to pass.

How is it possible to feel such a crazy combination of joy, sorrow, fear, elation, anticipation, apprehension and just out-and-out excitement that you get to put on a wedding?

You've never seen her this happy. Not even when you got her a new puppy at seven, or when she made a personal best time at swimming, when she nailed a Chopin nocturne or when her water polo team won a national championship. She was a one-girl Disney movie, bursting into raucous song at inopportune moments.

But you worry. You'll never have this beloved child all to yourself again. Her heart and her emotional life are now in the care of someone else, still a relative stranger—soon to be a strange relative, perhaps. You think about splitting holidays with her "other" family, you think about all the bumps and bruises that occur in even the most deeply loving relationship. She's taking a huge leap of faith, and all you can do is stand on the edge of the cliff and pray he'll be her soft place to fall.

2

START SPREADING
THE NEWS

Sharing the news with your family;
first decisions—what to decide
and what not to decide;
planning an engagement party

*I've got the ring on my finger
and the cell phone in my hand...
now what?*

ELIZABETH

I woke up the morning after Dave had proposed to me wrapped in a fluffy blanket in the honeymoon suite of one of Seattle's nicest hotels. The night had been absolutely dreamy—Dave and I had turned off our cell phones, ordered room service and spent all evening watching our favorite animated Disney films (a tradition that began in college when we realized we both knew every single word of every single Disney movie ever made). I had slept contentedly, smiling about the call Dave had allowed me to make to my mother the night before. He originally didn't want to share the news until after we'd had a night just for ourselves to enjoy being newly engaged, but he'd made an exception for my mom. Because, you know, I'm kind of obsessed with her. And she with me. And Dave knew better than to try to get in between that.

"Mommy, Dave just proposed to me!"

"What? He...what?! He DID?! YOU [smacking sound] LITTLE [smack smack] SNEAK!"

"What's going on, Mommy?"

"I'm beating your father for not telling me!" she laughed, giddy already with the news.

I excitedly recounted Dave's proposal to me, and told her aaaaaall about the ring.

"Take a picture!" she commanded.

"Okay," I said. "But we've gotta run because Dave's taking me to the Hotel 1000 for the weekend and they're waiting for us! I'll email you the pictures!"

"Great," my mom replied. Then her voice grew a little shaky. "Oh, baby, I'm so happy for you. I love you. And I love Dave, too! Can I say that? I love him! Tell him I love him! He's my new son!"

Laughing, I hung up the phone, snapped a couple of pictures of my new ring and of our beautifully decorated condo, sent them to my mom, then let Dave whisk me away for my weekend of blissful romance.

Waking up the next morning, I felt my stomach fill with excited butterflies. Today we would call all our friends and family and tell them our Big News! Yesssss!!! Dave was up with me, and as our cell phones powered up we eagerly chattered about who we would call first. His parents, of course, since they were still in the dark, followed by our grandparents, then our college friends...I was practically wetting myself with excitement.

As my phone turned on, however, it started having one of those cell phone seizures that happens when you've received a crap-ton of messages and it has to download them all at the same time. Dave's was doing the same thing. Odd, because we hadn't told anyone besides my parents that we were engaged.

Deciding to ignore all the messages, Dave called his dad at home. "Dad, last night I asked Wiggs to be my wife, and she said yes!" (P.S. Dave calls me Wiggs, invented to distinguish me from all the other Elizabeths, Beths, Lizzies, Betties, Birdies and Beppie McBeppersons. I think it's awesome. It makes me feel like I'm on a sports team.)

Dave was silent for a moment, waiting for his dad to react. I watched his face, eager to see the excitement that I was feeling. Instead, his mouth dropped into a moue of confusion.

"...oh," he said. "Oh, well, yep—it's true! We're engaged!"

Something felt wrong about this. How did his dad know already? I listened to Dave tell his dad how much he loved him and get off the phone. He turned to me and rolled his eyes. "Your mother," he said.

"What do you mean?"

"She made a slideshow with the engagement pictures you sent her last night before we left. So...everyone knows."

Okay, people. Let's take a time-out. Firstly, that is SO something my mom would do and I'm a dunce for not having seen it coming. Second, it did end up being a nice way for my extended relatives to find out about the engagement. But still, I was furious—and furious that I was furious on what was supposed to be the happiest morning of my life—that I had lost the chance to tell my loved ones myself. And Dave's poor dad, finding out about his son's engagement via a slideshow on the internet...not good, Wiggs girls. Not good at all.

We did get lucky, though, because Dave's mom was abroad and hadn't checked her email yet. When he finally got hold of her and told her we were getting married, I could practically feel bubbles of happiness popping through the phone and into my ear.

Can I just say, love is magic? Is that too cheesy for you? Sorry, but every bride-to-be feels it, the love and joy that oozes through the phone lines as you spread the news, far and wide. And in the end, despite my mother's Slideshow of Death (that's what I call it), we still spent a jubilant morning calling all our friends and gushing about how much we loved each other.

In hindsight, though, I'll say this to you future MOBs out there: ask your daughter who you're allowed to share the news with, and be cautious about who you tell. And brides: get ready to have to muzzle your mom if you want to control how your loved ones hear your news. That said, remember that this is an incredibly emotional and happy time for your mom and be kind to her. Don't ACTUALLY muzzle her. Just, you know, maybe wait until she makes that long-awaited journey to Timbuktu, or better yet, buy her the ticket. Perhaps you could convince your dad to temporarily disable the phones and internet. The goal is to make sure she doesn't start planning the engagement party with your future in-laws before they even have a clue that their son just decided to become a husband.

It might not happen this way to everyone. You might not worry about controlling the flow of information. Either way, the key is to know what you're up against. If your mom is wired to the world, you might want to have a word with her about discretion.

Or heck, maybe not. How cool is it to have a mom who gets *that* excited for you?

Now, it's easy to see the humor in the whole slideshow debacle. Dave was particularly relieved that we were still able to surprise his mom and his grandparents, and, as for me, I figure gossip spreads in my family like plantar warts on a wrestling team, so I never had any realistic expectation of keeping our engagement secret. Even for one lousy evening.

The part of our engagement I remember most fondly is the part I can take zero credit for: The "engageymoon" was Dave's invention, and it was perfect. The proposal was our own private moment, enjoyed together in our home, but I was so happy to get away from the mundane elements of everyday life—dirty dishes, noisy neighbors and mail needing to be sorted—to relax in bliss in our suite at the Hotel 1000.

Every couple's situation is unique. The most fun, successful and romantic engagements seem to happen when the couple gets engaged and celebrates in a way that feels true to them and their personal values. Trust me: I've made a study of this.

If you love a grand gesture and a big production, then that's how it should go down for you.

If you want to shout your news from the rooftops, grab a megaphone and go.

If skywriting is your thing, why not?

Spontaneity? Maybe he just falls to his knees while you're making him a tuna fish sandwich, and begs you to spend eternity with him.

Could be, the event will be triggered by an impending departure—he got into school somewhere. Or he's being deployed. Or a new job is taking him away from you...or you away from him.

All these situations happen every day, and not just in my mom's books. And they all work for the couple involved—again, the magic. The key is to be who you are...together.

I know whereof I speak. Just ask Dave. Before we were engaged, he had once caught me, by myself late one night, looking up videos of proposals on YouTube and crying my eyes out. Creepy? Yes. But he (correctly) deduced that I hoped to have our own engagement documented. Not for YouTube; that would have made the poor man's head explode. But for me, as a keepsake.

So for the sake of posterity, he set up a video camera to capture the proposal, and had an engagement photo shoot scheduled for the next morning. In the photos, you can see all the happiness and excitement of the first few hours we had together. You can also see the blissful ignorance written all over our faces; we had no clue about the can of gardenia-scented wedding worms we'd just opened.

SUSAN

I write the romances, but in real life, Elizabeth is clearly the romantic at heart. From the moment she realized Dave was the One, she fantasized deeply about getting engaged to him. Visualizing her dream was a preoccupation I certainly could understand, since that's pretty much what I do for a living.

On the other hand, it made me realize that my daughter and I were only at the beginning of a long list of our differences. This was a reminder of something every parent is bound to discover sooner or later: for every mom, there comes a point when you realize your child is her own person, not a miniature version of you.

There were a few surface similarities. It's true that I married my own college sweetheart, and also eerily true that he was also 6-foot-4 and athletic, never knowing his future daughter would one day manage

MEET THE PARENTS

You might get to choose your fiancé, but you don't get to choose your in-laws. I pretty much hit the jackpot with Dave's family—loving parents, cool brothers, down-to-earth aunts and uncles, grandparents who spoiled him (and now me) rotten. I got lucky.

Still, I laid some pretty awesome groundwork before I met them for the first time, just to be sure they understood how honored I felt to be their son's main squeeze.

When I met Dave's family for the first time, they didn't see me coming. Like a typical boy, Dave hadn't thought his parents would be interested in the fact that he'd finally met his Destiny.

I didn't want to completely freak them out, so I kept quiet about the fact that I was obsessively in love with their son and let them figure it out for themselves. I don't think it took very long. There were clear hints and obvious clues. Maybe it was that string of drool escaping from the corner of my mouth every time I looked at Dave. Maybe it was the fact that we both swooned and blushed every time our hands brushed. Or maybe Dave's mom noticed that I hadn't even touched the guest bed in their basement. Apparently, at dinner after I'd left their house, Dave got his nerve up and said to his parents: "You know Wiggs? Well, she and I are..."

"We know, David" was the response.

This is a perfect example of the difference between men

and women. My mother had known every single detail, down to the last adorable nose hair, about Dave since way before our first make-out sesh. Over the course of thousands of expensive cell phone minutes, he had been discussed, dissected, sliced, diced and remade in the image of Prince Charming. All Dave had to do was utter an incomplete statement: "You know Wiggs?" and his parents were savvy. Yeesh. I'll never understand it. Then again, I don't think it was the sentence fragment that clued Dave's family in. His parents always said (and this is a paraphrase from an actual conversation, so I'm not bragging) that they knew I meant something to their son because of the change that came over him once we were dating. Where he used to be one of the boys, playing king-of-the-mountain with leftover potstickers from last night's dinner, he now asked me what I wanted before serving himself. He grew gentler, more alert, more giving. I can't take full credit for this, of course. It was always part of his personality. But being around me, maybe, encouraged him to de-gruff his manly ways and let his sensitive side show a bit more. The effect was mutual, too. Being with Dave brought out my patience, my empathy and my desire to see my loved ones happy and relaxed.

So maybe he didn't need to tell his mom how special we were to one another. She probably saw it well before we did.

to find an updated version of him. But for me there was no proposal on bended knee, no photo shoot for engagement portraits (huh?), no luxury weekend getaway to seal the deal, no video record of the deed. This was back when the only thing you could see on video was a Betamax version of Jane Fonda in legwarmers, working out between glurgs of Michelob. Nobody proposed to anyone. We were in love, in school and penniless, and we simply assumed that getting married was the next item on the agenda for us.

So I never actually dreamed of a proposal. I simply dreamed of being married, and the engagement was the logical way to get from Point A to Point B. Not very romantic, I know, but it worked out well for us.

Remember, this was 1980, when the young folks of the world were busy shunning anything that smacked of tradition. The Alternative Era ended abruptly a year later, on July 29, 1981. This was the day the earth stood still for the die-hard romantics among us. Britain declared a national holiday, and in front of 3,500 invited guests, while an estimated 750 million people around the world watched on live television, the Prince of Wales and Lady Diana Spencer were married in St. Paul's Cathedral.

All of us who saw the pomp and circumstance can probably tell you where we were at the time. Most in the States were in our bathrobes, coffee mugs lifted in salute to the New Era. We were spellbound by the spectacle, the ceremony, the speeches, the music and, most especially—the *dress*. I'll bet you can still picture it in your mind— the yards and yards of sumptuous ivory taffeta and lace, a twenty-five-meter train bringing up the rear.

Never mind all the troubles and tragedy that ensued for the royal couple. All we knew back then was that a real princess was being launched, and weddings would never be the same.

So pervasive was the influence of this event that even our as-yet-unborn daughters would feel its echo, decades later. I know this was the case in our family. Elizabeth's determination to own her moment had its roots deep in the romance of that spectacular summer day in London.

While my vision for my own wedding was preoccupied with outcomes and goals, Elizabeth was determined to embark on the journey of a lifetime in her own way. I shunned the spotlight; she was comfortable at center stage. Fine, I thought. She's going to do it her way. My job would be to serve as air-traffic controller for all the incoming new people. Or so I thought. Little did I know, we were in for a bumpy ride.

ELIZABETH

I feared that introducing our families to each other might be like introducing zebra mussels into a pristine Great Lakes harbor. Toxic. Here's the thing: I've never actually been diagnosed, but I believe that I'm allergic to awkward situations. They give me rashes. Big, ugly red splotches that scream "I'm freakin' uncomfortable." And thinking about Dave's and my parents meeting for the first time gave me hives. After all, I had endeavored to keep my more crass tendencies a secret from the Maas clan, but as soon as they met my bawdy, irrepressible mother, I worried that my cover would be blown.

I did have an ace in the hole, however. In the first few months after meeting me, Dave's aunt was over at his house for dinner asking about his New Girlfriend. As you can probably imagine, one of the first things that comes up in conversation about me involves the fact that my mom is a romance writer.

On learning this, most people raise their eyebrows and commence psychoanalyzing me, the daughter of a novelist: Maybe she's a precocious vixen who is inappropriately comfortable with words like *bosom* and *shaft* (in actuality, my mother tells me her ears bleed when I make the slightest reference to sex). Maybe she's a spoiled princess, living in the lap of luxury and dining on bonbons as her loincloth-clad butler fluffs the mountain of silk pillows upon which she sits. (Reality: Writing is not the profession to take up if you want a private jet and an on-call masseuse.) Perhaps she's an airhead with the emotional depth of, well, a romance novel heroine who believes that a woman's true calling in life is to find a well-endowed, swarthy man to marry and serve. (Further Reality: my mother's heroines are smart, independent and usually pretty sassy, and second, we Wiggs women are boisterous and outspoken and don't need no stinkin' men to complete us.)

Lucky for me, Dave's aunt made none of these snap judgments.

It turned out that not only was she an avid romance reader, but she was a fan—*a fan!*—of my mom's books. I'd never met anyone who already knew of my mom! I knew she wasn't reading Susan Wiggs novels in an attempt to nose into our family. She just enjoyed and respected my mom's work. Finally! The books that had been the bane of my young adulthood were now making me look good!

Still, Dave's aunt was but one member of a giant family. How would the rest of his relatives react to my forthright, blustery mother and my gangly, Texan father?

The auspicious meeting would take place the weekend of our graduation from Pomona College. I set up a picnic brunch in the middle of a field on our campus and proceeded to chug Maalox in a vain attempt to settle my stomach.

Zebra mussels? What zebra mussels? Friends, I tell you, it was magical. Our parents instantly loved each other, our grandparents started joking around like old buddies. That initial mutual respect and affection for each other has remained throughout Dave's and my relationship, engagement and marriage, and looking back I'm glad I put special effort into making sure they had an enjoyable first meeting.

And, yeah, my mom told the story about the time I peed my pants during a ballet recital. And the one about the time I sat on a nail and got an infection on my butt cheek. ...and the time I tried to convince my eighth-grade English class that unicorns existed and the teacher called my parents in to make sure they weren't crazy. But Dave's mom didn't even bat an eyelash. Maybe my Eddie Haskell routine hadn't been necessary, after all.

Now, I realize that this isn't always the case. Some family meetings go over like a fart in church and sometimes nothing can be done about that. Still, you're the glue bringing these two families together, so you might as well set a pleasant tone...even if you know grenades will eventually be launched.

The same core truth will shine through—be true to who you are. Be strong in affirming your couplehood and trust your loved ones to love and trust you. It's remarkable how smart and supportive everyone will be when they get a load of your positive attitude. And it's incredibly easy to have a positive attitude when you're meeting the people who created your Prince Charming.

SUSAN

Many relationships in life are made according to your choosing. Your daughter's in-laws do not fall into this category. It's a completely random pairing. There isn't even a name for this relationship. "My child's in-laws" is a mouthful. For the sake of brevity, let's call them your co-in-laws.

You simply don't get a vote. Sure, she's bagged Prince Charming, and you couldn't be happier about that. But he did not sprout, fully formed, out of a petunia patch somewhere. He has People—a mom and dad, siblings, quirky uncles, aunts with good taste in reading material, uncountable cousins. And over the course of the wedding journey, you're going to meet all or most of them.

All I can offer is a bit of wisdom from my own wise mother: be nice and hope for the best. Advice, I might add, that applies to most of life's moments.

But you worry. These people are going to be in your daughter's world for the rest of her life. You'll soon be sharing her with them at holiday time, on vacations, get-togethers, celebrations through the years. You're going to be co-grandparents with them.

What if you're incompatible? What if you don't like them? Suppose their political views annoy you, or you disagree with their take on child-rearing or economics? Worse, what if they serve the stuffing *in the bird* instead of on the side? What if the only music they listen to is by Joe Pat Paterek and His International Polka Stars? What if they practice philately? Or hoard back issues of *National Geographic* magazine?

Or, worst of all, what if they're *perfect?* What if the dad is an esteemed lawyer and man of letters, and the mom is an eminent physician who runs marathons with her three flawless sons, practices at an HIV clinic and spends two months a year in a tiny African nation, treating indigent patients? What if the groom's parents are brilliant, witty, attractive, kindhearted and unassuming?

If that's the case, then they're my co-in-laws.

I am not making this up. The in-laws are saving the world, and the home team...? Well, we write romances and play golf. Clearly we were going to have to step up our game.

As it turned out, we didn't have to do anything but be ourselves, and the same held true for the groom's family. We came together, recognizing that our children were very likely going to be joined for life, and then it became easy to focus on the things we have in common— two adored children and high hopes for them both being the main glue to bind us.

Eventually we discovered more random common alities. Both moms are named Susan. They were married on June 28, 1980. We were married on June 27, 1980. The more we discovered about each other the more our hopes solidified—*the cause was good.*

The key to a successful first meeting, I think, is this: don't try too hard. Don't set up a big social situation filled with minefields of awkwardness and opportunities for one-upmanship. And for God's sake, don't overshare. Trust me, you'll do your daughter no favor at all if you talk about the existence of your husband's third nipple or your code names for some of her former boyfriends.

Instead, relax and above all, listen and laugh. And this bears repeating—be nice and hope for the best.

CHEAT SHEET

TOO BUSY BEING BLISSFULLY ENGAGED TO HAVE READ THE WHOLE CHAPTER? THIS ISN'T A HOW-TO BOOK (I'LL LEAVE THAT TO THE EXPERTS), BUT SOME OF WHAT I WENT THROUGH WAS FAIRLY UNIVERSAL...SO HERE'S YOUR CHEAT SHEET.

1. Once you start telling people you're engaged, get ready for news to spread like a virus. Make sure you tell all of the VIPs around the same time so you can avoid getting grief because your engagement popped up on Facebook before you told your family

2. Introducing your families to one another is only as scary as you make it. Even if you didn't win the in-law lottery, as I did, you can still put a little extra effort into making the first meeting pleasant and you might just be surprised by how well everyone gets along.

3

MONEY MATTERS

Navigating the wedding budget.
This is most likely the first time
you'll consider eloping

*You can't put a price tag on love...
but don't be surprised if
your mom tries to.*

ELIZABETH

Real talk, brides: your parents' wedding didn't even come close to costing as much as your wedding will. And your folks will likely exaggerate just how cheap their wedding was...a matrimonial form of "...when I was your age, I used to walk ten miles to school! In the snow! Barefoot! Carrying a set of encyclopedias!" In these cases, you could do what I did and go over your parents' heads to grandparents or other relatives who attended their wedding. My grammy was more than happy to dispel my mom's "$1,000 wedding" that took "one week" to plan. Still, weddings have become an industry unto themselves since our parents were putting on their love beads and getting hitched, so don't be surprised when you have to explain that you can't do a potluck reception at your local playground's picnic shelter.

A few weeks after Dave and I got engaged, I called my mom. As I picked up the phone, I didn't anticipate that our conversation would turn toward the wedding budget, an as-yet-unbroached subject. To be honest, I don't even recall how we even started to talk about money, which was mistake number one: Dave and I should have come up with a game plan before talking numbers with anyone else.

See, I thought budget would be the one point of the wedding that wouldn't cause any friction. And I had good reason (I thought). As we dipped our toes into the murky waters of wedding planning, my mom was always the one who came up with the most extravagant ideas.

"Where do you think we should go for our honeymoon, Mommy?"

"Oh, that's *easy*. The Château Frontenac in Quebec."

One Google session later, I opened the hotel's website. Except it wasn't a hotel. The word *chateau* should have been a clue. It was a castle. A glistening, expansive, $400-per-night-for-a-closet-with-a-twin-bed-in-it castle. Hmm, so for a ten-day honeymoon, that would be…$4,000 bucks on hotel alone. Factor in airfare, a couple of nice newlywed dinners (complete with champagne) and we were looking at a honeymoon that would cost upwards of $6,000 bucks. Not too shabby.

Okay, I thought. *So I guess I'm one of those lucky girls whose parents give her a platinum wedding.*

I could get used to this.

A few days later: "Mommy, what do you think we should serve as our main course for dinner?"

"Oh, definitely lobster," she replied. "With truffle oil. You need something special, but you should go with seafood because your father won't eat any animal he would own as a pet."

My pupils turned into little dollar signs.

"Mommy, what venues do you like for our reception?"

"Well, there's this resort about half an hour from our house—you should rent the whole thing out. And make sure you get the spa, too, so we can all get massages the day before!"

I liked the sound of this so much that I never stopped and reminded myself that my mother is *a romance novelist*. She spends her days spinning fictional tales for her heroines, sending them off to castles and lobster dinners and personal day spas without ever once having to worry about cost. Because NONE OF IT IS REAL.

She was treating our wedding like one of her books. And why shouldn't she? We were in the idyllic, brainstorming stage of wedding planning where the sky's the limit. I'm like one of those buxom babes whose ample bosom threatens to burst from its bodice as her open-shirted hero whisks her off into the sunset. It was only natural for my mom to mistake me for one of her characters.

But in my blissed-out, newly engaged state, I heard my mom's over-the-top ideas and figured she was giving me clues about how much dough my parents were ready to fork over for the wedding.

My search terms on wedding planning sites began to shift. Instead of "affordable A-line" I typed in "Oscar de la Renta silk tulle ball gown." "Seattle weddings under $3,000" became "eye-poppingly elegant Seattle wedding venues." "How to have a wedding without flowers" was replaced by "Ten-foot centerpieces with Swarovski crystals and custom lighting."

It was with this (okay, greedy) state of mind that I commenced planning the wedding. Again, I don't remember how we got onto the subject, but suddenly my mom said, "Would you elope if your dad and I gave you twenty-five thousand bucks?"

Um. What?

Okay, maybe she was kidding about the (gulp) elopement idea, but did this mean $25,000 was our budget? Really?

But...an Oscar dress (Mr. de la Renta and I were on a first-name basis by this time) cost $15,000. That would only leave...$10,000 for the rest of the wedding with nothing left over for the honeymoon.

In my mind, I saw Château Frontenac bursting into flames.

My lobster tail shriveled and became a saltine cracker adorned with a squirt of Easy Cheese.

My towering, glittering centerpieces toppled over with a deafening crash.

Twenty-five thousand bucks wouldn't even cover a fraction of the wedding I had cruelly been led to imagine.

I tried to buy myself time by asking the question I thought I already knew the answer to. "Why would you want us to elope, Mommy? Don't you want to see your only child get married?"

"Well, honestly, Elizabeth, it might be a good idea to focus on practicalities. You know that. Most people who get invited to weddings would rather send a gift and not have to go and pretend to enjoy gummy buffet food and cheesy DJ music."

"But...what about the lobster?" I whimpered.

"Lobster?" she said. "Ha! Can you imagine how much that would cost? A nice lobster dinner's gonna run you a hundred bucks a head... if you have 150 people at your wedding, that's fifteen thousand bucks just on *food*. That's insane!"

Was someone playing a practical joke on me? Hadn't *she* proposed the lobster?

I tried a different approach. "Well, twenty-five grand would be great for eloping, but we want to have a real wedding. I mean, we don't have to spend a hundred bucks a head, but...I mean, $15,000 for food *and* drink really isn't that much."

Oops.

Brides, take heed: never, ever tell your self-employed, freelance-writer mother whose royalty payments only come twice a year that any sum of money "isn't that much." For that matter, don't say those words to *any* mother. She didn't get to where she is by ignoring the realities of budget.

The conversation spiraled downward from there. At one point, my mom said $5,000 was a perfectly adequate amount for a wedding, to which I replied that I would need twenty times that amount to have the wedding I wanted. That's right—I heard myself requesting $100,000 for my Big Day in the middle of a conversation that started out with her offering to pay me off for eloping.

I mean, really. My parents had generously paid my tuition for one of the most expensive private undergraduate institutions in the country. I blithely ignored the fact that putting me through said college meant that they had to hold off on traveling the world and buying a new home—one they had been saving for since before I was born. In their minds, they were financing a degree that would exponentially improve my life. Setting that aside, I stupidly told my mother that an ostentatious wedding would definitely improve my life!

I tried telling her that the average cost of a wedding in the U.S. was close to $30,000, to which she responded with the oldest mom trick in the book: "I don't care what everyone else is doing. I'm your mother and I say you can do better than everyone else."

She reminded me that $100,000 spent on *one day* amounted to a down payment on a starter home. Two years' tuition at business school. A small fleet of new hybrid cars with all the trimmings. When I replied that I had no immediate plans to purchase a home, I'd get a scholarship for my MBA and I didn't need a car, she upped the ante and figured out that a hundred grand would feed four hundred children in Ghana for a year.

And what could I say to that? She was right.

I got off the phone with her that day feeling shaken. Suddenly, my dream wedding felt impossibly out of reach. Worse, though, I experienced a frighteningly adult sensation of personal responsibility and conscience. My wedding fantasy had turned me into someone I barely knew—a person who was grasping and entitled, a person who had forgotten that any sum of money my parents gave us for the wedding was a *gift*.

The sum to underwrite the platinum wedding represented a life-changing fortune to 99 percent of the world's population, yet I had assumed that my parents would gladly fork over whatever it took to give their baby a lavish wedding. I searched deep, trying to justify the lobster, the gown, the chateau, the whole glittering dream and I couldn't make myself do it.

And that was exactly what my mom wanted.

She's a wily one, right?

In hindsight, I can see that she wasn't as concerned about the money as she was about my values. She didn't like the idea that her child had grown into the sort of person who would spend money on a party instead of saving it for something that really mattered.

And I have to give myself credit: If left to my own devices, I eventually would have come to my senses. Even if money were no object, my inner voice of reason would have hauled me back from the brink. I never would have been able to pull the trigger on ten-foot-tall, crystal-encrusted centerpieces, knowing that the money spent on them could be used for something much more lasting and meaningful in my life or the lives of those around me. (But let's not kid ourselves, Dear Readers: I would have taken that Oscar de la Renta dress in a heartbeat. I said I was frugal, not crazy.)

A couple of weeks later we sat down as a family, my levelheaded father and manfully brave fiancé with us, to discuss the wedding budget like sane people.

The conversation was still unpleasant. It never feels good to ask or be asked for money, whether it's $100 or $100,000. We argued a bit, and I got defensive, but eventually we hammered out a sum that everyone could live with. At the end of the day my parents agreed to give us $20,000 to spend however we wanted, and if our wedding ended up costing more than that, we would be on our own to figure out how to pay for it.

Not to ruin the ending of this book, but I eventually *did* have the wedding of my dreams. Dave and I set our priorities, item by item. We made a list of the most important wedding elements to us, and allotted our spending accordingly.

Remember that Google search I mentioned earlier about "how to have a wedding without flowers"? At first blush, the very concept seems inconceivable, doesn't it? When a girl dreams of a wedding, she imagines imported Casablanca lilies, themed end-of-aisle arrangements, a bouquet of rare orchids trailing from here to Omaha. Here's a real quick way to get the bloom off the rose: Crunch the numbers. Flowers for a wedding can run from $2,000 to $20,000 and beyond. The lower-cost ones are not earth-friendly, the environmentally conscious ones cost the moon, and at the end of the day, everything winds up in the trash.

Surprising as it seems, flowers didn't pass the smell test. The Sri Lankan Kadupul blooms were relegated to the bottom of our priority list, along with six miles of aisle swags, urns of topiary clipped to resemble our favorite Disney characters and ribbon woven from the delicate wings of endangered Bengali moths. My bridesmaids ended up carrying three large, yellow mums each. They looked beautiful, nobody complained, and I didn't lose sleep over spending six grand on something that I honestly didn't give a hoot about.

As we were ~~fighting~~, er, figuring out exactly how the money would be spent, something happened to me and Dave. Our ~~knock-down-drag-outs~~, er, lively debates were actually long, intense, relationship-testing discussions that ultimately revealed important details about our inner selves to each other. And let me tell you, as uncomfortable as this can be, it's not a bad thing to make sure you're on the same page about the merits of imported, jewel-encrusted boutonnieres. In the end, your bond will strengthen as your vision and purpose take shape. Which is a fancy way of saying that Dave and I sort of decided how to spend our budget...and in the process, we laid the groundwork for future financial

Here are some of the inspiration and reference websites I used to ground the wedding decisions I made—and these are just the tip of the iceberg. Google your heart out, bride!

http://costofwedding.com
http://www.theknot.com
http://www.weddingbee.com
http://snippetandink.blogspot.com
http://www.marthastewartweddings.com
   (especially their seating chart tool)
http://www.sites.google.com (for our wedding website)
http://www.theweddingreport.com
http://www.greylikesweddings.com
http://stylemepretty.com

decisions in our lives together.

Note to brides: ***do not skip this step.*** Work on your wedding as a couple. It is a microcosm of many discussions you'll have as a married couple, and you might as well get your differences out in the open now.

I can't say it was easy, because by the time we got a hard number out of my parents, my heart was already set on some fairly pricey ideas. Still, I managed to fit everything I wanted into the budget my parents gave me.

Let's get real, people: there's no unilaterally pleasant way to hash out your wedding budget. If you can pay for it yourself, do it. Don't stress your parents out about it. And if you need their help, don't forget to be grateful for whatever amount they give you—even if all they're able to provide is love and support.

Just make sure you don't get roped into the conversation before you're ready with some hard data, a clear idea of what you're going to ask for and an open mind.

And never forget to heed the immortal words of the Notorious B.I.G.: "Mo' money, mo' problems."

SUSAN

When it comes to giving advice about money, I am not the one to ask. Remember, I'm the one in the pink-tinted shades, writing novels that are meant to transport readers to the realm of fantasy. And I'm the person who ditched a perfectly stable and predictable teaching career in order to pursue my writing dreams. "Pursuing one's writing dreams" is often a euphemism for "being unemployed" or later, once you've found a publisher, "living in subsistence-level poverty."

I have known the uncertain merits of measuring the backseat of the car to see if it's actually conceivable that a family could live there after eviction. I've eschewed entering my books in prestigious award contests because I needed the entry fee to buy groceries. Oh, and those phony-looking blank checks that come in the mail with your credit card statement? Guess what? You really *can* write them to the IRS.

As you can see, budget and finance are hardly my thing. Passion, not practicality, is the fiction writer's strong suit.

Long-term survival in this business does, however, train even the most passionate among us to be cautious when it comes to spending money. So when your adored and newly engaged daughter comes to you and says she wants to spend six figures on her wedding day, feel free to take a moment.

Take two moments. Knock yourself out.

Dealing with the wedding budget is a crucible for family values. How much is enough? How much is too much, and how—outside of a small brown plastic pill bottle—do you find the balance?

I don't recall exactly what my own wedding cost. I do remember that my dad wrote a single check to the Always and Forever Wedding Chapel, and he didn't even break into a sweat. Our "reception" was a gathering of friends and family at my parents' home and we had a sheet cake from the grocery store around the corner. However, I do concede that I was not the girl who fantasized all her life about being a bride. I fantasized about writing that bride's story, again and again. If someone had threatened to take that dream away, she would have had a fight on her hands.

Here's where I want to remind you—your daughter's wedding is about *her* dreams, not yours. And who are you to deny this person her dreams? So what if you want her to spend her wedding budget on a 401(k) plan or a down payment on a home? Take a deep breath, step back, give her a lump sum you're comfortable with...and let go.

My husband likes to say water finds its own level. You hope that level is not so deep that everyone ends up like the people in steerage on the *Titanic*. Chances are, you'll come up with a plan that makes the bride happy. How you get to that point is a mysterious process involving, to borrow an apt phrase, a searching and fearless moral inventory of your finances, your marriage, your emotions and your conscience.

I know what you're thinking: *I'd rather have a root canal.*

But I also know you'll do the right thing. Take a deep breath, take a step back and set priorities.

Warning: the wedding industry is a Vast Dove-Wing Conspiracy that exists in order to shake you down like a two-bit pickpocket. It's easy to get swept into a vortex of wanton spending in which you—a hitherto reasonable individual—are brainwashed into thinking you cannot possibly pull off a wedding without horses dyed to match the bridal party colors, saffron-infused Kobe beef wrapped in Maine lobster tails and sprinkled with gold leaf and Beluga caviar, matching Louboutin pumps for the bridesmaids, a flyover by the Blue Angels and letterpressed toilet paper.

Do me a favor and stay in touch with your Common Sense Fairy. You know her. She's that smart Inner Girl who has reeled you back from the precipice all your life. She'll remind you to take a step back, do your breathing and embrace your right to the line-item veto. Heed her well.

Ultimately, the goal is to celebrate this incredibly happy couple and to launch them into a beautiful new life. Trust me: you're not doing them any favors by simply agreeing to their every whim. You want to have a meaningful ceremony followed by a memorable party. It's very liberating when you think of things in those terms.

Chances are, you can just say no to the letterpressed toilet paper.

CHEAT SHEET

I KNOW, I KNOW, YOU MEANT TO READ THE WHOLE CHAPTER BUT THEN YOU GOT INTO A GIANT KNOCK-DOWN-DRAG-OUT WITH YOUR MOTHER ABOUT YOUR WEDDING BUDGET. HERE'S YOUR CHEAT SHEET:

1. No matter how well-off your parents are, compared to you and the rest of the country, any amount of money they fork over for your Big Day is a gift. Treat it as such. Don't set yourself up for failure by feeling entitled to any sum, however small, from your folks.

2. You know why you don't need to freak out if your parents don't give you much money? Because there's a lot you can do on the cheap. Sit down with your fiancé, make a list of priorities and figure out which elements you can toss out of your wedding completely. For me, it was floral arrangements. Does music make you go "meh"? Think about replacing your ten-piece band with an iPod.

3. If you keep your eye on the prize (no, not the $0,000 cake—your relationship with your future spouse), you won't be thinking about the corners you cut on your wedding day, anyway.

4

SPACES AND PLACES

Choosing your venue, and why
having a simple backyard reception
turned out to be the most complicated
and impossible idea we addressed
in planning our wedding

*Mom, how do you feel about having
Porta Potties in your backyard?*

ELIZABETH

HOMETOWN WEDDING RUMBLE

Mommy really wanted the wedding at home, and even lobbied like a teamster-with-lipstick about it. It didn't bother her in the least that traveling to the tiny, wet, green island where I grew up was going to be problematic for out-of-town guests unfamiliar with the watery hell that is the Seattle ferry commute. She thought nothing of cramming up to two hundred guests onto the groaning deck in her backyard for canapés of salmon spread and Dixie cups of Cold Duck. She was quite certain that, even though the town rolls up its sidewalks at sundown, we would not hear a peep of complaint about the loud partying until midnight. I might have mentioned this before—my mother spends her days with fictional characters who iron out all of life's problems by page 386.

Here's the thing: Dave and I decided early on that we wanted to make our wedding as easy as possible on our guests. Yes, the day was all about us, but our guests were the ones making the hike out to Seattle and buying us extravagant gifts. (Well, MOST of them were buying extravagant gifts. Those who didn't were permanently put on the "cheap postcard during the holidays" list. Not that I'm bitter or anything.) Essentially, my hometown was difficult to get to and had no easy, affordable and roomy venues. Sound simple? Try telling that to your mother who has just offered to shell out the equivalent of the average person's annual salary on your wedding.

All I can say is, stick to your guns. If you're adamant, be adamant with a smile on your face, and make sure it's not a rictus of ridicule. Get married in a place that you and your partner love. Period. Trust me: your mom will learn to love it, too—even if she refuses to admit how awesome it was until the whole thing is over.

Dave and I were devoted to Seattle and had found a venue that we thought was beautiful and fit our budget. Court in the Square was located in a quaint historic neighborhood just south of downtown. It was an entryway between two old brick buildings during the day, but on the weekends the six-story glass atrium served as an event space. Its retractable roof let the sun in, catching an infinity-style fountain at the far end of the room. The two buildings that formed the north and south walls of the venue maintained their exposed brick and lush, green window boxes. Fifteen-foot-tall live potted trees were interspersed around the room, each of them on wheels so they could be relocated to make space for different event layouts.

Oh, and did I mention that it cost only seven hundred bucks to rent?

It was perfect.

More perfect than my hometown.

That was a hard conversation to have with my folks, and in the end we never really did reach an agreement—a few weeks before the wedding, my mom was still saying things like, "Well, if you'd had the wedding at our house, this wouldn't be an issue..."

But that's one of the things you learn as you plan your wedding: you can't please everyone, not even the most important people involved. You have to learn to disagree without having the whole process come to a standstill. The Native American Hopi tribe requires a bride to grind cornmeal for three days in her mother-in-law's kitchen while the groom's aunts attack her with mud. I knew my refusal to have the wedding in my hometown was a bit of a slap in the face to my mom (at least, that's what she thought), so I worked to make sure she had a chance to feel at home during the wedding weekend. The cool thing about a

wedding is that it gives rise to ancillary celebrations, like brunches, barbecues and happy hours. They're entirely optional but a good way to extend the joy beyond the Hi-Bye crush of the wedding reception— and you can use them to throw your mom a hometown bone.

Her main point throughout the hometown wedding battle was that her house was a beautiful, free venue that would be incredibly easy on my whole family. When I asked how she felt about having Porta Potties for two hundred people in her backyard, she blithely shrugged and said, "They can come inside and use our guest bathroom!"

Thinking back to other weddings I'd been to and the state of the bathrooms after the bridesmaids had guzzled one too many lemon drops and unleashed a stream of citrusy vomit on the tiled floor, I gulped. I tried explaining to her how difficult it was going to be to find parking, to calm the neighbors when things got noisy, to keep her crystal stemware from being shattered on the concrete patio, but she wouldn't be swayed. I tried trumpeting the benefits of our chosen venue, Court in the Square: close to home, accessible for all our guests, ample parking, beautiful atmosphere, airy space...but to no avail.

Then she sent this email to Dave and me:

From: Susan

To: Elizabeth, Dave

Subject: Wedding thoughts (long)

> [Side note: I should have been tipped off by the *long* appended to the email subject line, a grim indicator of the drama I was about to plunge into headfirst.]

Dear Elizabeth & Dave,

Your dad and I want you to consider holding the festivities here on the island where you grew up. It's a place with emotional ties, something that resonates more than a rented venue in Seattle. Friends and family will come to your wedding regardless of distance and convenience, even if it means camping out in the state park.

I know you're determined for this to be a comprehensive celebration with the people in your life, including your beloved but always a bit difficult grandfather. Regardless of what a wedding planner may tell you about handling guests, your grandfather will need to leave early (I won't go into the reasons for fear of scaring off the groom). Your dad will accompany him back to the island and that will be the end of Grandaddy *and* your dad for the day. Sorry, but that's how it will play out.

Court in the Square is trendy, but there are many other island venues to explore, including the country club, the golf course, the local park, the community theater house, the gazebo at the state park, the winery, the rose gardens and more. And I still think about how taken you both were with the new church on the island. There was something in your faces as you looked around...

The ultimate goal is to be happily married for good. We all want that for you. But whatever you decide, let me know you've given this due consideration. Sorry to Dave for bringing you into the family drama. Poor Dave!

OK, end of manifesto. Let me know your thoughts.

Love,

Mommy

She's good, huh? This is what happens when your mother writes for a living. She takes up her pen against you—and it cuts straight into the most tender, vulnerable spot in your heart. She had some valid points, as well as some that were not so valid. For instance, Court in the Square is gorgeous and in the end we spent very little on décor. And did she actually suggest that our guests consider camping? But she ended up being correct about my grandfather needing to leave early—and on the wedding night, I was sad to have to say goodbye to my dad well before the reception ended. I'm glad that she made me think about those things ahead of time, because in the end I would have been dramatically more upset if I hadn't been expecting it.

But you can tell how she felt. I didn't know how to respond, so I

ignored the manifesto and hoped someone else would deal with it.

And—what do you know?—I had a fiancé who was already on top of it. With no prompting from me, he sent a measured, perfect response that left my mom feeling respected, listened to and accepting of our plans.

From: Dave

To: Susan

Cc: Elizabeth

Subject: RE: Wedding thoughts (long)

Dear Susan,

Thanks for communicating everything to us. I don't have some castle-in-the-clouds idea of how this thing has to go. And right now it's hard to wrap my head around rethinking the venue from thousands of miles away during my first year of law school. I just want a wedding that brings together our two families and friends to celebrate what is hands-down the most important event of my life.

Since college, Seattle is the only place both of us call home. Court in the Square is green, open-aired, full of old exposed brick, versatile, spacious, and the feel of six-story glass ceilings is hard to beat. It's the awesomest [sic] reception venue we saw.

A reception on the island would require guests to drive afterwards, which will worry me. Even if someone has only one drink before leaving, there's still a liability [OMG, my budding lawyer man!] that doesn't exist in a city crawling with taxis. I personally like the idea of an event where the generations meet and celebrate together, but I imagine all the grandparents will trickle out early... We'll do our best to make it as easy as possible for both of our families.

Our wedding will be an overwhelmingly happy and positive experience for me even if it rains on us and all the guests end up in jail for the night. Everything else aside, it will be the day we start our own family, and that won't be affected by the logistics.

Your thoughts are important to me (us) and we want to make our families happy!

—Dave

Wow. He's good, too. Any guy who can say *awesomest* with a straight face is a keeper, for sure.

My mom and Dave both had great points, and ultimately we decided not to completely rethink our wedding. Dave and I were both happy with the venue we'd already chosen. Still, I understood how important it was to my parents to host our family and friends on their home turf, so I asked Mommy to have a welcome barbecue for our immediate families and wedding party the Thursday before our wedding.

The barbecue went off without a hitch and was the perfect way to reunite with relatives I hadn't seen in years. My mom got the hosting bug out of her system, and we eased into the wedding weekend, content with the way things played out.

CHEAT SHEET

DID YOUR FANTASIES ABOUT GETTING MARRIED AT WINDSOR CASTLE DISTRACT YOU FROM YOUR READING? HERE'S YOUR CHEAT SHEET:

1. Okay, yeah, you do get the final say. So use your power wisely. Don't force a venue down your mother's throat. Gently express how perfect your chosen venue will be for you and your honey— and, if you can, find a way to honor her wishes, too. Ask if she would like to host a family-only event in the week before the wedding at a venue of her choice.

2. If your mother (or other similar wedding elf) does not go gentle into that good night, be sensitive. Your wedding is a big, emotional day for her, too—and it's only natural for her to want to be in her comfort zone.

3. When in doubt, sic your fiancé on her.

5

THE ONE

Not the man, silly—the dress

Dress shopping and the hunt
for the last frock you'll ever
wear as a single gal

ELIZABETH

My quest for the dress began with a mistake. Dark forces were at work, inexplicably drawing me to the swankiest bridal salon in Seattle, a place that would eventually prove to be more toxic than the set of VH1's *Rock of Love*. (For the uninitiated, that's one of the finest reality shows on television, in which a troupe of strippers with balloons for breasts compete for the lust of aging rock musician Bret Michaels.)

In fiction, such places are guarded by rabid, three-headed dogs, but at the Swank Salon (names changed to protect the bitchy), Cerberus had been replaced by a burbling replica of the Trevi Fountain.

My mom, my future bridesmaid, Molly, and I skipped happily through the flower- and crystal-encrusted door into a hippodrome-sized, airy room filled with every beautiful wedding gown I ever imagined. I'd never given much thought to the infinite possible shades of white, but here I was, jaw on the floor, confronted by the whole pale spectrum gleaming in satin and silk, lace and lamé. The shop was designed in the round, with layers of dresses lining the outer walls of the space like a cupcake wrapper, tasteful doors with hand-painted French signs tucked away behind the racks. Each door was unique, and promised a cozy and beautiful nook for trying on the dress of my dreams.

But the center of the store was what really made me need the crash cart.

There, raised about three feet off the chic navy-blue carpet, was a glowing Lucite runway. Plush ivory chairs sat at either end of the runway, understated yet unspeakably elegant, with crystal champagne glasses on low tables and bottles of Dom Perignon chilling in monogrammed ice buckets. A discreet video camera was set up at the far end and live images of the empty runway appeared on flat-screen televisions throughout the shop. French music from the movie *Amélie* filled the air, just soft enough to add to the ambience without interrupting the rustle of chiffon and tulle.

I felt a string of drool dribble from my lower lip and plop on the old tank top I wore.

"We'll give you a DVD of all the dresses you try on, so you can show anyone in your life who's not here today," cooed voice behind me, dripping with sweetness.

I turned around and stared down at the waif of a salesgirl who had materialized behind me like a silent-but-deadly fart.

"I'm Brigitte," she said.

Her black hair was meticulously teased into an edgy, bouffant-style ponytail. Her eyes were expertly rimmed in kohl black eyeliner, adding drama to her pale, elfin face and petal-pink cheeks. She smiled at me, revealing a row of perfect teeth that were whiter than any of the dresses she peddled. She wore black skinny jeans and a beige cashmere sweater that wrapped luxuriously around her small form as though it had been made for her. When she moved, a collection of chic bangles on her wrists made a soft clanging noise, calling attention to her perfectly manicured, purple-black fingernails. She probably weighed about the same as one of my calves.

In short, she was a bride's worst nightmare. She pretty much looked like a model, except she wasn't tall so I couldn't convince myself that she was one of those girls who's too tall to love (I get judgmental when I'm feeling intimidated). I quickly realized that I would be trying on my dresses in front of her, which didn't bode well for my self-esteem. Standing next to her, I felt like the offspring of a cow and an ogre. The cellulite on the backs of my thighs tingled a warning signal at me, as if to say, "Get out while you still have your dignity!"

But I didn't listen. The siren call of the runway in the center of the enormous shop was too much for me. I sucked in my gut, plastered a confident-ish smile on my face and introduced myself.

She looked me slowly up and down, one delicate hand twirling a silky strand of dark hair. She frowned slightly, her impeccably waxed eyebrows coming together in an expression of thoughtful confusion. I could practically hear what she was thinking: What could possibly disguise those flabby arms without accentuating her pear-shaped hips? (This was before I had gotten in shape for the wedding, after all. But still.)

"What do *you* think would look best on you?" she asked me. The emphasis on *you* made it seem like she very much doubted my fashion sense. I mean, I was wearing old yoga pants and a shirt with a built-in bra, but isn't that what most gals would wear when planning to spend an entire day trying on dresses?

I'm just glad I'd been planning my wedding gown from the moment I popped out of the womb, because I had a firm answer for her: "I want the biggest ball gown you've got. Strapless."

She smiled, her glossy lips turning up even as her eyes lingered on my upper arms as if to remind me that a strapless gown would do nothing to hide the lard-filled wings that flopped from my biceps whenever I moved.

I reminded myself that from her point of view, in which Kate Moss represented the ideal body type, my slightly undefined triceps muscles would appear offensively large. And, yes, I did need to do more dips at the gym. But I was a former college athlete, and I knew how to get myself toned. Sure, I could stand to lose ten pounds or so, but I tried to remember that I wasn't as grossly obese as her expression implied. A strapless gown would look lovely on me. I might just need to live on celery and water for a month before the wedding.

I smiled back. "Yep," I said. "A strapless ball gown."

"Great!" she chirped. "And what budget are we working with?"

As she asked, she began to usher my mom, Molly and me to a corner of the store where I could see deliciously poofy-looking skirts dangling beneath delicate-boned bodices.

"Uh...I was thinking maybe around a thousand bucks? I guess I could go up to fifteen hundred if it was perfect enough. Does that sound about right to you, Mommy?" I looked at my mom and Molly, hoping that I hadn't just named an offensively outrageous sum of money.

"Or *less*," my mom stated, seemingly unfazed by this evil bird of a woman.

The heroin-chic salesgirl stopped in her tracks. I could practically hear the soles of her patent-leather ballet flats screech on the floor. With a poisonous look in her eyes, she rounded on me.

"I'm not sure if you know how much a *high-fashion dress* costs in an upscale shop like ours, but you *really* need to reconsider how much you're willing to spend on the *most important gown you'll ever wear*." The bangles on her wrists jangled as she stabbed her tiny hands through the air to emphasize her point.

Suddenly, she looked down and stopped midsnarl. I saw her eyes light on my mom's robin's egg blue Christian Louboutin pumps (bought for 90 percent off their usual $900 price tag at Nordstrom Rack). The sight of high-end shoes seemed to calm her.

"I mean," she tittered, taking on the tone of a concerned friend, "you wouldn't want to pass up the gown of your dreams just because you're letting a *silly little thing* like budget get in the way, would you?"

"I...I..." I stammered.

I think I was suffering from temporary insanity due to couture vapors, because if I were treated this way in any other circumstance, I would have flashed her my pleasantly plump middle finger and gone out for a burger. But here, in this tulle-draped shop that looked as though it had been spun from my little-girl wedding dreams, I was speechless.

Brigitte saw my moment of weakness and knew she had me. All she had to do was get past my last line of wedding defense—my mom.

She looked down at my mom's shoes as if to gather strength from their signature red soles, then tried a new tactic: "Mrs. Wiggs, I can see by your ensemble that you're a woman who knows fashion. You must see how *tragic* it would be for your daughter to wear a less-than-perfect gown on the day of her wedding."

My mom, in an uncharacteristic moment of gullibility, seemed to waver. I'm guessing this resulted from the cloying scent of gardenias wafting through the air from the multitude of floral arrangements adorning the shop.

"Well," she said, "I suppose we could look at a couple of *slightly* more expensive gowns...but nothing over two thousand. I'd be shocked if we can't find something beautiful for such a price."

The words *more expensive* seemed to bring Brigitte back to life. Invoking a salesgirl's selective deafness, she ignored the *slightly* part of my mom's response and promptly took us on a whirlwind tour of tulle-and-satin heaven. She seemed to float around the shop, hoisting piles of gowns that must have weighed more than she did and transporting them to a dressing room that resembled Marie Antoinette's boudoir.

She ordered me to strip down to my grundies (that's grandma-undies, to those of you who are still convinced that G-strings are comfortable). It only took me a minute (and a glass of Dom Perignon) to forget my jiggly abs and flabby butt as dress after beautiful dress slipped over my head, each more stunning than the last. Brigitte's fingers flew, fastening rows of minuscule hook-and-eye button closures with machine-like speed; she was able to fill my mom's and Molly's champagne flutes with little more than a threatening glance. Finally, when I thought I had been through every ball gown the store had to offer, Brigitte opened the door to my dressing room. "I saved the best for last," she breathed, a glint in her eye.

With the wily skill of a crack dealer, she produced a breathtaking whisper of couture for me, reverently placing the cloudlike garment on a gilded hook on the wall. She whisked aside my privacy curtain without so much as a "Hide your eyes" to Molly or my mom. "You'll want to see this one, ladies," she said.

I tried to pull a Venus-on-a-half-shell maneuver with my hair and my hands, hiding my lady bits as much as possible, but my pathetic attempt at modesty was unnecessary as all eyes in the dressing room were on the silk tulle layers of the gown. As it swayed on its hanger, I noticed subtle crystals peeking through the folds in the voluminous skirt. Swoon.

Employing a device that looked like a giant crowbar, Brigitte forced me to pour my pre-wedding-diet hips into the size 0 and had the buttons fastened down my back before my flesh could burst free. I was disconcerted. Vaguely humiliated, even. I felt like a sausage whose casing was too small.

I turned, disappointment on my face, to Molly and my mom. "I look like a joke, don't I?"

Molly's eyes were like saucers. "Oh, Wiggs," she said, her eyes full of emotion.

I knew it. I knew it! Brigitte's hard stares at my winter-soft physique hadn't simply been the result of her lifelong goal to be able to hide behind a toothpick. Sure, she hadn't actually said anything about my body, but I knew what she was thinking, and she was right. Now Molly thought so, too.

I should just get married in a bathrobe. I could never pull off the ball gown I'd been dreaming of since I could say "printheth" in my toddler's lisp.

I glanced at my mom and saw her clutching her heart.

Okay, it wasn't that bad, was it?

Was I really giving my mom heartburn with my over-the-top wedding dress preferences?

I turned slowly to look in the mirror and survey the damage. There, standing before me, was exactly what I'd been fantasizing since I was a little girl.

The dress was...perfect. The skirt drifted to the floor, forming a large bell with a four-foot train that would have made Disney animators jealous. The bodice nipped in at the narrowest part of my waist and suddenly I found myself glad for my curvy hips. The warm ivory color of the delicate tulle set off creamy peach tones in my skin, causing my blue eyes to take on a cerulean hue. My hair, pulled carelessly back and slightly frizzy from the frenzy of dress changes suddenly seemed carefree and romantic. A soft sweetheart neckline, bordered by glinting crystals, gave me nontrashy cleavage (how's that for a miracle?), and huzzah! My arms looked slender.

The skinny bitch got it right. This dress was The One.

I happily skipped about the entire store, jumping up on the runway and flouncing to and fro, checking myself out in the mirrored walls and squealing like a contestant on *The Bachelor.*

I looked Brigitte in her flat eyes and said, "This is it. I'll take it."

In a flash, her face came to life and her expression changed to what can only be described as a barracuda with a plump, juicy goldfish in its sights. "Great," she cackled, steepling her fingers (seriously, she really did steeple her fingers). "This one is $12,000. Plus tailoring, fitting, prewedding storage, dewrinkling, steaming, refitting, day-of fitting, postwedding storage." She might as well have added postdivorce repurposing for good measure.

I'd been waiting for my mom to burst into tears when I found the dress of my dreams. And she did, but I'll never know if it was the sight of her little girl in the bridal gown, or the price tag that broke her down.

My lower lip began to tremble. Twelve *thousand* dollars? But that was almost my entire wedding budget! Wildly, my mind began to race, trying to divine a way for me to afford the gown. *You could have this dress if you fed your guests squirt cheese on Rye Crisps and downgraded the music to a kazoo quartet,* I told myself.

You could offer to moonlight here as a salesgirl and work off some of the cost, I thought. I looked at Brigitte and realized I'd never make it in the underworld.

Then I was hit by a lightning bolt of genius. *Run!* I heard the voice in my head screaming. *Run now! While she's not expecting it!* As my leg muscles tensed, I was already calculating how much jail time I could get for stealing a $12,000 dress. I edged toward the door, trying to recall exactly where I'd parked the getaway car. And then I caught another glimpse of myself in the mirror—this time from across the room, where the fine details on the dress (including the designer's name embroidered into the tag) weren't as apparent.

You know what I looked like?

A bride. A bride in a big, white dress. A young, excited bride who was glowing with happiness over the prospect of decades spent with her soul mate.

The expression on my face—the one I'd been wearing since I met Dave, actually—was the most stunning part of my ensemble, and I knew then that any gown I chose for my wedding day would simply be icing on the cake. But it wasn't the cake. I was.

Because, folks, here's the reality: a big white dress is a big white dress. It doesn't matter if it was designed by Coco Chanel or Koko the Ape. Other than the occasional Rachel Zoe addict, no one is going to be able to tell the difference. Cheesy as it sounds, a happy bride's smile will shine more brightly than any Swarovski crystal ever could.

So go ahead and wear your dress (or skirt, or pantsuit, or bikini, or skort or whatever bridal outfit you choose) like it came right off a Parisian runway. The only thing people will remember (if they remember anything besides the color) is how you glowed with joy. And maybe some will remember the cut (including you), so if you want a ball gown, get a blasted ball gown because it's the only chance you'll have to wear one without looking like you're in a costume.

If you find your dream gown and it's in your price range, more power to you. I wasn't so lucky. But that dress set the bar. As I happily flounced out of the snobby store, taking with me any commission Brigitte could have hoped to earn, I had to thank her for one thing: she gave me exactly what I was looking for—a vision quest. I had been within reach of The Dress, and all that remained was for me to find something equally gorgeous with a price tag that wouldn't require me to sell a kidney. From then on, my dress shopping would be efficient and focused. I would only consider ball gowns, and only those under a thousand bucks.

Everything happens for a reason, my mom says. Looking back, I can see now that without the encounter with Brigitte, I never would have ended up at the next shop.

Later that afternoon, my mom, Molly and I went to lunch in the quaint neighborhood of Wallingford in Seattle. Molly spent a good part of the lunch convincing me to eat more than a piece of lettuce, reminding me that I was not actually a candidate for world's largest woman and that I was *definitely* not allowed to let Brigitte and her skeletal aesthetic make me feel bad about myself. My mom simply said in her most matter-of-fact voice, "You can't trust a girl who weighs less than the purse she carries."

As we walked out of the café, I glanced across the street. Nestled along a rosy pink wall, four shop windows displayed mannequins in long, white gowns. Above the door to the small shop, a humble black awning read, I DO BRIDAL.

I'll be honest with you. I always pictured finding my gown in a place that oozed upscale elegance. My dressing room attendant would serve my mom and bridesmaids teacakes and champagne as I tried on dress after beautiful dress, emerging from behind a billowy silk curtain to stand on a dais in front of the women in my life as they lounged on a pillow-soft couch. Even after my experience with The Harpy Formerly Known as Brigitte, I figured I'd find another store with a similar atmosphere—and more reasonable prices.

I DO BRIDAL looked a little...homemade, compared to my fantasy.

This is where it came in handy to have an insanely practical mother and a down-to-earth bridesmaid with me.

"Wiggs, why don't we try that shop?" Molly asked. She knew a thing or two about finding wedding dresses in unlikely places. Her own wedding was a mere two months away, and she would be wearing an incredible raw silk A-line gown she'd found in an eastern Washington quinceañera shop that sported a window display of neon-green prom dresses.

My mom piggybacked onto this: "Yeah, it looks like the exact opposite of the last place. It will be a breath of fresh air."

Feeling grumpy and tired, I turned up my nose. "I'm not going to find what I'm looking for in *that* place," I sneered. "'I Do Bridal?' How about 'I Do Saks Fifth Avenue?'" I huffed, thinking myself clever.

But Molly and my mom already had me by the wrists.

They bodily threw me through the door. The first thing I saw was a tattered, industrial-style carpet littered with small threads, sequins and buttons that had fallen off sample dresses. In one corner stood a fake-gilt fainting couch for the moms. The air was musty, and as I looked up, I saw why: on three racks crammed into a space roughly the size of Dave's 1980 two-door Volvo sedan, a mountain of wedding dresses threatened to explode from their tight confines like my back fat from a size 0 bodice.

I stifled a groan and mentally vowed to appease my mother by trying on three token dresses before I made a beeline for the car.

"Hi!" chirped a cheerful voice. Emerging from the nest of dresses like a bridal gnome, a small woman beamed at me. She looked...well, like me, only Asian. Young, with an average build, wearing comfortable jeans and a T-shirt, her glossy black hair pulled back into a low ponytail. She wore no makeup and had a genuine smile, and as she reached out to shake my hand I noticed a small but beautiful solitaire engagement ring on her finger. "I'm Bridget," she said.

I immediately liked her. I looked around to see if someone was playing a joke on me—she really was the non-French version of the snob from the first store. My mom and Molly smiled at each other, knowing how serendipitous this was. It seemed like a sign.

I resolved to keep an open mind—even though the entitled bride-devil on my shoulder kept whispering sweet nothings in my ear about

expansive dressing rooms and Oscar de la Renta gowns. I calmed myself down by promising to make an appointment with Saks immediately if the dresses here were lame.

I told Bridget that I wanted the biggest dress she had. She con-
gratulated me on my engagement and asked me a couple of questions
about the wedding, my dress budget, my style and, most importantly—
what my fiancé wanted me to wear. "Obviously, he doesn't get the final
say," she giggled, "but you want your future husband to love the dress
almost as much as you do, right?"

She had a point. On the runway earlier that day, Dave's opinion
had been the last thing on my mind as I fretted over price tags and
imaginary pockets of fat on my arms.

"He always tells me I'm his very own Disney princess," I said. (Um...
and Dear Readers, if you ever meet Dave don't mention that to him—
he'll tell you he only likes *The Lion King* and *Tarzan*, Disney's more
manly selections.)

Bridget grinned. "I have the perfect dress for you."

She turned on the heel of her canvas sneaker and prepared to dive
back into the mass of dresses crowded along the far wall of the store.

"Wait!" I said, just as she heaved a row of hangers off to the side.
"Is this...this *perfect dress*...under a thousand bucks?"

"Of course!" she said. "Honestly, we don't carry that many gowns
over your budget."

I heard my mom's audible sigh of relief at this, but the greedy
devil appeared again on my shoulder, hissing, "How can a *cheap* dress
look anywhere near as good as the one you had on this morning?" I had
to admit to myself that the gown this morning had set the bar pretty
high—and it had also set a reference point on price. I could feel myself
anchoring on $12,000 as a figure that indicated a level of beauty and
quality that less expensive dresses simply lacked. Then I caught Molly's
eye as she helpfully held aside a pile of chiffon so Bridget could unearth
the dress she had in mind for me.

Molly's gorgeous wedding gown, the raw silk number that made her look like a blond Audrey Hepburn, had been inexpensive—and it had all the bridal bells and whistles, including subtle crystal detailing at the waist, intricate ruching on the bodice and beautiful tailoring that would hold up a few decades from now for her own daughter's wedding.

I brushed aside the selfish devil on my shoulder and stepped into my teeny dressing room. Bridget appeared a moment later, arms full of glittering tulle.

"Most girls don't even want to try on this dress because it's *such* a ball gown," she said, panting from the effort of carrying it. "But for a girl who has Prince Charming waiting for her at the altar, this is The One."

She plopped the dress on the ground, skirt first, and it stayed standing like a mountain of bridey-ness. She unzipped the bodice (I reminded myself it was okay to have a bodice with a zipper instead of buttons or ribbons) and asked me to step in. I closed my eyes and took the plunge—literally. I misjudged how much fabric I had to step over to get into the dress and found myself clawing at the cloth walls of the dressing room, trying to keep my balance without shoving my grundies into Bridget's face. She reached out, grabbed my hand and guided me to the patch of floor buried beneath the layers of ivory netting.

As she zipped me up, I kept my eyes on the floor. I didn't want to see myself until I was standing with my mom and Molly.

Bridget took the back in with industrial-sized clamps. Turns out that at most bridal salons, where you're not expected to be built like a twig, the sample dresses are typically size 10 to 14 to work for any body type. I already felt better about myself. We didn't need any Wiggs-sized crowbars to shove me into *this* gown.

I stepped out of the dressing room, arms held out slightly to accommodate the wide skirt that fell from my hips, and looked at my mom and Molly.

I'm sure you've already guessed what happened.

This time, both of their eyes filled with tears, and I knew they were the good kind.

I stepped up to the trifold mirror and peered at myself.

Would you believe it—this dress was friggin' *better* than the one I'd tried on that morning. It had a more classic line and hit my hips exactly below their natural curve, making me appear as deliciously feminine as any Disney princess. The bodice was covered with silver crystals and embroidery, which, seen from a few steps back, made me shimmer. And my boobs! They looked great! Perky, a little larger than they naturally are, but not like giant melons or anything (I'll take whatever I can get). The skirt was made from layer upon layer of ivory tulle, forming a wide, swishy circle that swirled around my feet as I moved. A chapel-length train floated on the floor behind me, the top layer embroidered with tiny flowers.

It was the dress of my dreams. It was too good to be true.

I gulped. "Okay, how much does it cost?"

"This one is $750."

"Seven hundred fifty...dollars?" I asked, gaping.

I looked at my mom, who was managing to keep herself together. She gave me a small, firm nod. Sha*zam*.

On my wedding day more than a year later, people couldn't stop complimenting me on the dress, I felt glorious about myself and Dave needed CPR the minute he saw me.

My mom, I'm forced to tell you, knew I DO BRIDAL was a good karma shop as soon as we went to the front of the store to purchase the dress: at the main counter, writing up orders with calm efficiency, was a woman who shared a story about her own daughter's wedding gown. She was a mother, too. And when there's a mom in charge, you can't go wrong.

SUSAN

When Elizabeth found the dress I was thrilled—but not a bit surprised. The moment I saw it, I thought, "Of course."

Why? Because I'd known what the dress would look like since she was five years old. She started drawing pictures of herself as a bride back then, and in every picture she drew, she was wearing this exact dress, practically down to the last detail. There was always a crystal-encrusted bodice surrounded by yards and yards of sparkling tulle, a veil worthy of Maria in *The Sound of Music* and high-heeled dancing shoes.

The most important attribute of the dress, as any little girl will tell you, is that it must bell out gracefully when she spins around. Every time Elizabeth tried on a dress or even a nightgown, she would spin like a dervish. "It swirls," she would say. "It swirls!" If the swirl factor was not present, the garment would go straight back to the rack.

The dress she found had swirl. It had crystals. Beading, tulle, you name it. When she spun around, that sucker swirled clear to Cincinnati. It was, for sure, The One.

The only missing detail was the groom. As a tiny girl, she wasn't picky. In fact, for the longest time, she thought the word was *broom* and decided it was a perfectly good dance partner. The groom might be a large plush toy with button eyes, or our aging Golden Retriever. Sometimes she'd rope in an actual kid. I remember a boy she called Stinkypants in preschool who was willing to stand there like Bambi in the headlights while she twirled around him.

The one thing that never changed was that dress. Twenty years later, the vision came to life in a tiny bridal shop in Seattle, and it was well worth the wait.

It passed the spin test. It *swirled*.

So that's the good news. The bad news is, the mom has to wear *something*. And okay, I'll just say it. Reality bites. You know which reality I mean—the one that glares at you with the unblinking clarity of a three-way mirror in the dressing room.

Most of us don't spend our time in the limelight on a day-to-day basis. So when it smacks you upside the head that you're going to have to look fabulous on your daughter's Big Day, you start to fret. You look in that mirror, illuminated by the least-flattering light ever to beam down on a bulge of cellulite, and fretfulness sets in.

While your size-2 daughter is being outfitted as the Princess Bride, you're feeling like Jabba the Hutt. You start thinking about the thousands of pictures that will be taken, and all of a sudden liposuction doesn't seem like such an unreasonable proposition.

Time for another little consultation with your Common Sense Fairy. Remember that although you're an important part of this day, you're not the most important part. And here's another little tidbit. Do yourself a favor and go look at some photos of people's weddings. The bride is *always* beautiful, isn't she? And the bride's mother looks just magnificent, doesn't she? Even if she's, um, gravitationally challenged and wearing a chiffon monstrosity of a dress, she looks great in the pictures. Here's the key—a photo of someone who is happy and having a great time is always going to look good. Genuine emotion trumps cosmetic surgery every time.

However, you do need a dress. But I'll tell you what you do *not* need. You do not need a chiffon monstrosity. You don't need a drapey muumuu or a bell-sleeved tunic covering up your arms. You don't need something edgy and loud and fashion-forward that calls attention to itself. And you don't—God forbid—want to clash or compete with the groom's mother.

Here's what you do want—you want to look age-appropriate but stylish enough. You want to feel comfortable even six hours into the festivities. You want to *dance*.

I'm a little out of my depth, offering style tips. As a writer, I tend to spend long hours alone in a room, wearing a sweatsuit, fuzzy slippers and headphones. (Sorry about that visual.) I pretty much have the fashion sense of a gas station attendant. And I'd rather watch moss grow on a barn roof than spend a day shopping.

But I'm a quick study and I know how to listen and go to the experts. I'm also a champ at web surfing. So my own personal quest for the dress started there. Once the princess picks her colors, head out on a web safari.

Stick to the palette. This doesn't mean you have to match. You simply don't want to clash. If you're as challenged as I am, check the color wheel. Or better yet, call up your most fashionable friends and ask for their advice.

Steer clear of dedicated bridal stores. No offense to your local "Gowns'R'Us" outlet, but the mother-of-the-bride dresses tend to be, um...dowdylicious, to coin a term. Nothing screams "I hate my Teutonic butcher's wife arms" more than a claret-colored, bell-sleeved tunic.

Try some off-the-beaten-track shops and designers. Try picking the brain of your daughter's fashionista bridesmaid who works at Nordstrom. Once you narrow down your list to a few options, go ahead and order a few (make sure the store has a fair return policy because you probably won't hit paydirt the first time out). And run them by the princess. Trust me: she has better fashion sense than you do. I ended up wearing a fun but age-appropriate dress in a subtle silk moire print by a newish designer called Leifsdottir. The aforementioned fashionista even found it for me half off at Bloomingdale's, and I felt great in it, even with my brutish arms showing.

Here's a little shopping secret I'm happy to share. You know those shoes? Those incredible, cute, danceable shoes? (Hint: Google "Hey Lady" shoes: www.shopheylady.com.) They do *not* make you look fat. So go ahead and indulge.

Reminder: tell the groom's mom what you're wearing. Only in bad romantic comedies do the moms show up in the same who-wore-it-better gown.

CHEAT SHEET

TOO BLINDED BY REAMS OF WHITE SATIN TO READ THE WHOLE CHAPTER? HERE'S YOUR CHEAT SHEET:

1. I already said it, and I'll say it again: *a big white dress is a big white dress.* Remember this when you feel a tug in your gut toward that haute couture gown that will put you in the red.

2. Go to the upscale bridal salon—but do your due diligence afterward and see if you can find an equally beautiful dress that isn't overpriced just because your dressing room was the size of a tract mansion.

3. The most beautiful part of your wedding ensemble will be the girl wearing it.

6

THE VERY IMPORTANT PEEPS

Choosing the attendants,
dressing the attendants,
putting gratitude before attitude

ELIZABETH

As soon as you get engaged, people start peppering you with questions. "Have you chosen a date?" "What does your dress look like?" "What colors are you going to have?" And, possibly the most rife with danger, "Who's going to be in your wedding party?"

Brides, I don't claim to be a wedding expert, but I will give you this one command: when someone asks you who your bridesmaids are (even if the asker is your conjoined twin sister), say, "I'm just so excited about being engaged that I haven't even thought that far ahead!" Do yourself a huge favor and practice saying this into the mirror, over and over again. "I'm just so excited about being engaged that I haven't even thought that far ahead!"

Because, trust me, it will come in handy.

Now, I was lucky because I ended up having the best bridesmaids I could have asked for. Each girl represented a different part of my life and a different, lasting friendship. Joelle was my cousin, my rock, my unconditional support. Melissa was the childhood best friend, who had seen me through my most awkward adolescent years, my first kiss and my first heartbreak. Lucy was my college roommate, who had talked me down from the ledge of undergrad dating. Molly was my best friend, the caring, unjudgmental soul who loved me fiercely. Lindsey, another friend, kept me grounded, colluding with me in my neurotic need to plan and organize all our friends' lives. Aubrey, my stylish and also-engaged friend, didn't mind if I called her at 3:00 a.m. to bitch about a fight I'd had with my mom over our wedding budget. They were all there for me on my wedding day as nobody else could have been, and I love each of them like the sisters I never had (not that I'm bitter about being an only child or anything, MOMMY).

That said, I was a total klutz about choosing my bridesmaids. Almost immediately after Dave said, "Will you?" and I said, "Yes." See, two days after Dave and I got engaged, we met my parents for brunch to celebrate and show off the new rock gracing my finger. And at that brunch, like any doting mother of a recently engaged gal, my mom asked me who I would have in my wedding party.

Well, okay, she didn't exactly ask.

Of the many skills she possesses, none are so potent as her uncanny ability to sound like she's making a request when in actuality she's issuing a command. Woe be to the maiden who attempts to defy her orders, as I did that sunny spring morning.

"So I'm assuming your girl cousins will be your bridesmaids, right? You know, blood is thicker than water. The only woman I speak to on a regular basis from my childhood is my sister, and since you don't have sisters, cousins are your next option. Right?"

See how she did that? It's verrrrry tricky: first, she states the command as an assumption she has already made, because, honestly, who could even think of any other possibilities? But then she softens the assumption by tacking on a very gentle "...right?" Then, before you can respond, she steamrolls further ahead with an argument that she's obviously already researched and outlined (it's not for nothing that she's an incredibly talented writer, even about things with which she has no experience). This time she made the strategic move of referring to her sister, my favorite aunt, Lori.

I was pretty much a goner.

And here's the thing: she had only the best of intentions. Even then I could see that she was simply drawing on her own life experiences...and, well, maybe allowing her love for my cousins to cloud her opinion the teensiest bit. My mom prides herself on being a world-class auntie. She often says it's her favorite role in life—all the fun of being a mom and none of the responsibilities. Some aunts send their nieces a T-shirt or a coin purse at birthday time. My mom hires a personal stylist and takes them to Nordstrom. So I shouldn't have been surprised that she instantly assumed I would embrace the idea of surrounding myself with the darling girls.

Even more complicated was the fact that I dearly love my cousins, too. Cassidy is a precocious twelve-year-old who gives better relationship advice than women twice her age. Caitlin is a willowy seventeen-year-old, an award-winning ballerina with a quiet smile and doe eyes. They're lovely, incredible girls who make me puff up like a tick with familial pride every time I think of them.

Of course my mother had thought this out.

She also knew, with a mother's intuition, that I had already decided on Joelle, my eldest female cousin, to be my maid of honor. Joelle is a year younger than me, but she's the closest thing I can imagine to a sister. We love each other, have a crazy Vulcan mind link and have managed to last a quarter of a century without killing each other despite being constantly compared to each other. Sure, she got the bigger boobs, while I ended up with the blonde ringlets. She laughs inappropriately when she's nervous, while I make crude sex jokes. She's a whiz in the chemistry lab, while I can write English lit papers in my sleep.

But despite our superficial differences, we have a connection I can't describe. She is me, and I am her, and when we're old ladies together we will be the only two people in existence to know exactly what it was like growing up as we did in our tiny, zany, hilarious family.

So, kudos to my mom for figuring that out before I told her. Joelle would be my maid of honor.

And in my mom's mind, the other female cousins logically followed suit.

Here's where my command to you should have come into play. I should have said to my mother, "You know, that's a great idea and I'll have to give it some thought once I decide to start choosing my wedding party. Thanks for the input."

Here's what I actually said, "Um, no."

Whoopsie-daisy.

I went on to dig myself an even deeper hole, reminding my mom of all the wonderful women in my life. And it's true: as a veteran of two intense sports teams and an amazingly fun college, I have a giant list of gals who merited the title of bridesmaid. I mean, I'd spent so much time with some of these ladies that our, ahem, cycles had synced up. If that's not friendship, I don't know what is.

More importantly, while I love my younger cousins to death, I thought they might not understand the importance of being a brides-maid. On my wedding day, while I was chugging an unhealthy amount of champagne and cussing like a sailor, I didn't want my teenage cous-ins to be the ones in charge of cutting me off. When I threw off my robe and got fully naked to step into my wedding dress, I was pretty sure the twelve-year-old wouldn't want to be the one to hold my boobs in place while her sister buttoned my corset. And I had a feeling it might technically be breaking the law to ask a minor to hold my skirt up while I took a nervous pee in the ladies' room during the reception.

But again, all this could have been said later, once the newness of the engagement had worn off a little. And once my mom had a chance to retract her claws of control a wee bit.

My mom and I both believe that we are unquestionably correct, all the time, and that we are each cornucopias of mind-blowingly good ideas, the likes of which most other people would kill for. So you can imagine what it's like when we disagree.

The concept of being wrong is, for me, the same as thinking about my parents' sex life: I prefer not to imagine it and when I do, it makes me shudder. Ack, did that make you think about your own parents in the sack? Gross. Let's try another analogy: for me (and my mother, actually), wrongness is like the square root of negative one: it simply doesn't exist.

So there we were, two days after Dave had proposed to me, having our very first mother-daughter wedding fight while our king crab omelets turned cold and rubbery.

Dave and my dad, meanwhile, sat agog at the table, the blood slowly draining from their faces and their eyes growing to the size of saucers. They were beginning to realize that allowing my mom and me to plan the wedding together would be like putting two wet cats into a potato sack. One of the men—I don't remember which because I was seething with fury by the time this happened—eventually suggested that we not make any decisions about our wedding party until we thought more about what kind of wedding Dave and I were going to have.

"It doesn't change the fact that cousins should be bridesmaids before the people you get drunk with every weekend, Elizabeth," my mother griped.

"It also doesn't change the fact that this is *my* wedding and I can do it however I like and I don't *care* what you say," I snapped back.

Good lord, we were really on our game, weren't we?

But we got over it. That's the good thing about my mom and me: we can fight like, well, two wet cats in a potato sack, but the next time we talk, we're back to being best friends again.

Ultimately, the bridesmaid choice wasn't really about who put on the matching dresses and dyed shoes. It was about the meaning attached to the gesture. For my mom, it was all about family. For me, it was about the bond of friendship. Our job was to figure out how to give us both what we wanted, not to win an argument. So I did something my touchy-feely liberal arts education taught me: I found a creative solution.

A few weeks and a couple of thousand internet searches later, I found the answer to my bridesmaid woes—the *junior* bridesmaid. Who knew?

According to Wikipedia, *A junior bridesmaid is a girl who is clearly too young to be marriageable, but who is included as an honorary bridesmaid.*

Further digging online taught me that junior bridesmaids are treated much the same as regular bridesmaids, but with the understanding that their role carries fewer responsibilities. And fewer tequila slammers.

With Dave holding my hand for support, I called my mom to tell her my idea: my younger female cousins would be included in the wedding as junior bridesmaids, walking down the aisle at the head of the wedding party, and then sitting with the family through the ceremony. I also gave them the special job of carrying single white flowers to give to our mothers and grandmothers as they reached the altar.

By golly, my mom snapped that idea right up, and before she could obsess over it for another second, I called up my aunt and told her the news.

Mommy had one thing right: they were overjoyed. They happily and sweetly embraced their roles. On the wedding day, the two girls showed up at the bridal suite with their hair perfectly styled, their makeup carefully done, their angelic faces wreathed in smiles. They added something so special to the occasion that now I can't imagine doing it any other way. It was exactly the right choice to include them in my wedding party.

I just wish I had kept my trap shut when my mom first proposed the idea of having them as bridesmaids.

Now that I had my two junior bridesmaids and my maid of honor in place, that left an unidentified number of open spots in my wedding party. The bridal books will tell you to find a memorable, fun and meaningful way to invite your girlfriends to be bridesmaids. I kind of wish I'd read that part before sticking my foot so far into my mouth I couldn't see straight.

Here's how to ask your friends to be bridesmaids: have a plan, know how many girls you will have in your wedding party and don't ask anyone until you've decided who each of your maids will be.

You've probably guessed that I screwed the pooch on that.

The first girl I asked was my childhood best friend, Melissa. Shortly after Dave proposed to me, she asked who my bridesmaids were going to be. Caught off guard, I stammered, "Well, YOU, obviously." Gah! Think about it: if you were going to be a bridesmaid, would you want to be asked like that?

In a more graceful world, I would have said, "You know, Melissa, I haven't thought that far ahead yet." And then I would have taken her out to lunch and made a cheesy but totally awesome speech about how much her friendship meant to me and how I would be so happy to have her stand up there with me on my wedding day.

But, oh boy, it gets way worse from there.

I knew I wanted my friend Lucy, a former college roommate, to be a bridesmaid. So I instant messaged her. During work. I actually have the conversation saved in my computer:

me: so i was thinking...

Lucy: hold on one sec, my manager is coming over

me: okay

[ten minutes pass]

me: ...you there?

Lucy: i'm here, sorry

Lucy: what were we talking about?

me: well so i have a HUGE favor to ask

me: you can totally say no if you want

me: like, seriously

me: like, if you don't want to say yes, you WILL NOT hurt my feelings

me: because i understand that this is a huge favor

me: ...a HUGE, HUGE favor

me: but

Lucy: do you need money, wiggs?

me: god! no!

Lucy: oh okay because it's totally cool if you do

(Let's pause for a moment so I can clarify a few things. First, I have never asked a friend for money. Good lord. I think Lucy must have been thrown off by the way I introduced the subject. Second, gag me. What was I trying to do, talk her out of being in my wedding? I showed the grace of a hippopotamus trying to dance *Swan Lake*.) Anyway. The conversation continued:

> **me:** no! i was just going to ask if you wanted to be a bridesmaid!
>
> **me:** but i know that being a bridesmaid is a burden and it's fine if you'd rather just come to the wedding as a guest
>
> **Lucy:** aw, wiggs, of course i'd love to be a bridesmaid!
>
> **me:** really? :)
>
> **Lucy:** yeah! that's so sweet of you to ask me!
>
> **me:** omg i'm so excited!!! i just knew that you had to be up there with me
>
> **Lucy:** wow, i'm so happy! hey, i have a meeting right now but i'll call you later, k?

Ugh. Reading that now makes me realize how lame I was when I asked Lucy. If she didn't know me better, she probably would have thought I was trying to get her to say no. Again, that would have been a great time for me to call her up, since she didn't live in the same city as me, and have a conversation about being a bridesmaid when she wasn't juggling work meetings and roaming, predatory managers.

And then there were Molly and Lindsey, my two best friends. We had been close in college, but we fell in friend-love when we all ended up in Seattle after graduation. They were the first non–family members I called when Dave and I got engaged, and both of them reacted to the news by screaming so loudly with happiness that the speaker on my cell phone was forever damaged.

They were my rocks throughout the bridesmaid fight with my mom, counseling me and encouraging me.

Yes, Dear Readers, I did say that *they* listened to my agony over deciding who to have in my wedding party. My two best girlfriends.

One day, as we were out having coffee together, I said to both of them, "You know, I really wish I could ask you to be bridesmaids, but you're the only two people who I don't have to play politics with. I know your feelings won't be hurt if I don't ask you, because you understand that no matter what you're the most important friends I have."

Ohhh I wish I were making this up.

How awful is that to say to a person? "I love you so much that I feel comfortable pretending to love someone else more."

Of course, they were incredibly kind about it and didn't point out what a jerk I was. Both of them responded that they understood, and that I shouldn't feel bad.

When I told Dave about this conversation, he looked at me as though I had just burped up a talking salamander.

"Uh...Wiggs...those girls are the only ones I was sure you'd ask. They're your best friends!"

"I know!" I whined. "So they can handle the rejection better! They know it's not purrrrsonal!"

As soon as I said it I could hear how wrong it sounded.

But, again, instead of doing the right thing and taking them out for mani-pedis before asking them on bended knee to be my brides-maids, I waited until we were tipsy one night at our local dive bar and slurred, "Hey, so, I think I probably want you guys to be my brides-maids. But if I end up feeling like I have to ask someone else, I know you won't mind stepping down, you know? Because I can be totally honest with you. You know? I love you guys."

Sometime after that I got up on a pool table and did an interpre-tive dance to "Cold as Ice" by Foreigner.

And you know what sucks? I never retracted that clause about asking them to step down if I ended up feeling obligated to ask some-one else. At the time, I drunkenly thought I was just being "real" with them. You know, like when a reality show contestant says, "I'm not fake. I'm keepin' it real."

Like true friends, they were both overjoyed and excited to be bridesmaids, and to this day neither of them has ever busted my chops for being the worst bridesmaid-asker in the history of the world.

I deserve to have my chops busted, though, don't I?

The final person I asked to be my bridesmaid was Aubrey, a girl I hated in college.

Let's pause for a second so I can tell you how most of my female relationships have evolved: first, I meet a new girl. Immediately, I draw comparisons and find something to envy about her. In Aubrey's case, it was her fierce model-like good looks and infuriatingly petite body. Quickly, that envy turns to hatred, so I go around talking trash about the girl until someone calls me on it and then I'm forced to stew in my own outrage, knowing deep down I'm a jealous hag and nobody feels sorry for me.

The good news is that this unfortunate tendency has forced me to develop some world-class amends-making skills.

Eventually, I came to see that I needed to get over myself and acknowledge Aubrey's fabulosity—both as a stunningly beautiful girl and as a devoted friend.

When Dave and I got engaged, she was one of the first to congratulate me and immediately sent me a card she had designed and printed with her 150-year-old letterpress machine.

Okay, let me just say that again. *She designed and printed a card for me on her 150-year-old letterpress machine.* She's such a classy broad.

Now, after screwing up the previous bridesmaid invitations, I finally got it right: I hand-wrote a letter to Aubrey telling her how much she meant to me and how thankful I was to have her in my life. I packaged the letter *with* her size-less-than-0-but-I-love-her-anyway bridesmaid dress and shipped it in a flat box on which I had written REQUIRED WEDDING ATTIRE ENCLOSED. It was a lovely gift, if I do say so myself, and I know that she'll keep the letter forever.

She probably would have loved the package I sent even more if I had not put it in the mail exactly three weeks before the wedding.

That's right, folks. Three weeks.

See, Dave and I were engaged for sixteen months, and a lot can change in that amount of time. As the wedding drew closer, Aubrey became one of my most important supporters and I slowly began to see how much I needed her in the wedding party. She had become more than a friend to me; she was a sister.

But then I hemmed and hawed for, like, two months.

Who does that? God, I suck.

Lucky for me, she took my ineptitude like a champ and never let on that I had forced her to jump through all the bridesmaid hoops (arranging transportation, getting dress alterations, etc.) in a fraction of the normal amount of time.

Hindsight being 20/20 and all, I wish I could go back and send cool little packages to my girls or take each one out to lunch and pour mimosas down their throats. You know what, I might just do that right now.

But, Dear Readers, despite my terrible maid-asking skills, I'm going to go ahead and toot my own horn about how I treated my maids once they were asked. Let's call a spade a spade: I was a pretty great bride, as far as my girls were concerned. I tried my damnedest to remember that they were cherished friends throughout the whole process, and they paid me back by keeping the champagne flowing, fixing my updo when it began to droop, enthusiastically clawing for the bouquet when I threw it and staying on the dance floor until their feet bled. And—the most important test of all—they're still my friends today. So, given what an awesome bridesmaid experience I had, here are my thoughts on Zen and the art of bridesmaid wrangling:

A bridesmaid is not, as the title implies, there to serve you—she (or he) is your support. Historically, bridesmaids and groomsmen dressed alike and stood next to the couple as they said their vows to confuse evil spirits who would curse the marriage. They were willing to tackle malevolent demons for their friends' happiness. Today, many brides seem to see their maids as dress-steaming, Band-Aid–fetching slaves. But think about it: your maids are your friends. They've watched you fill a toilet with upchucked peach mojito, and they've been on boob-watch for you when you wear a sparkly, nipple-skimming top to dinner. They will answer the phone at 3:15 in the morning when you've thrown your engagement ring down the stairwell and are seriously considering entering a nunnery, and the next morning they'll bring you a soy chai latte (your favorite), look you right in the puffy, red eyes, and tell you you're pretty. They've been your cheerleaders, your shoulders to cry on and your trusted sisters. Be grateful to have your peeps up there with you to witness your union with your soul mate. And, you know, attempt to show that gratitude.

By asking your wedding party to stand with you, you're honoring the friendship you have with each of them. Keep that in mind when you're choosing their outfits and outlining their duties. I found cute dresses for my maids at Target, and at $34 a pop, I was able to gift them to my girls—and when we took them to the seamstress for alterations, she thought they were Vera Wang gowns. Booya! And on my wedding day, I made sure to take time with each of my bridesmaids to let her know how much it meant to me to have her there.

When Aubrey and Lindsey left the cocktail hour to help me remove my veil, I told them how much I appreciated it. When Lucy hugged me goodbye for the night, I let her know that her calming presence had gotten me through the more stressful parts of the day. When Melissa showed up for portraits, having executed her own runway-worthy hair, makeup and styling, I made sure to tell her how gorgeous she looked. When Joelle cried all the way through the ceremony, the signing of the marriage certificate and her toast to me, I cried with her and told her how much I loved her. And when Molly used her arms as a forklift to help me lower my bride-ass onto the toilet without soaking my dress, I thanked her before I emptied my bladder of four glasses' worth of champagne. I'm proud I remembered to be grateful.

So here you sit, flush with engagement bliss, ready to gather your women around you and assign each of them a special role. Just remember that they already know how much you love them, and they love you, too—and they're not going to hate you if you take your time as you decide what parts they will play in your wedding. They'll be patient with you, just as you would with them. And, uh, try not to ask them via text message, or two weeks before the wedding, or in the midst of a drunken rampage. Shudder.

SAYING ADIEU TO YOUR SINGLEHOOD

Most brides and grooms still practice the tradition of a bachelor and bachelorette party. If you're anything like me, you have spent many a happy hour with girlfriends fretting over what sorts of trouble your betrothed's stupid college buddies are going to get him into. Maybe you've called his big brother who's in med school to make sure he knows how to detect and diagnose the signs of alcohol poisoning. Or maybe you've disastrously attempted to issue an ultimatum: "Go to a strip club and you'll need to find yourself a new fiancée." Perhaps you've stood over him and dictated an email to his bachelor party attendees informing them that since he's going to be a lawyer when he grows up, he won't be partaking in consumption of any illegal substances OR streetwalkers. Or possibly you designed one T-shirt for every day of his bachelor party, each with a different menacing photo of your face and a caption saying some version of, "My future wife will kill you if you touch me."

...Oh. Was that just me? Whoops. To put it bluntly, I had my grundies in a twist long before Dave started planning his bachelor party. Looking back, I had nothing to worry about, but for the record, I'm still glad I printed those T-shirts for him. They were hilarious. I sneaked them into his suitcase the night before he left and made his best friend reveal them to him once they got to the hotel.

I also lucked out, though. Instead of a typical trip to the Vegas strip, Dave wanted to go to Alaska. During the summer solstice. To run a marathon.

Yep. And eighteen of his friends agreed to come with him. They also agreed to wear costumes—Daisy Dukes and suspenders, head-to-toe neon spandex, a clown costume…

Yet I still worried. Would they find some hairy-armed, gun-slinging moose huntress to do a pole dance for him? Would the guys force Dave to drink bourbon through a beer bong and then throw him down the side of a glacier?

It's really hard to get out of that paranoid mindset, even if you know and love your fiancé's friends almost as much as he does. Unfortunately, you might just have to spend the weekend feeling uneasy. But here are a couple of things you can do to ease the tension:

- Have an open discussion before he goes about what sort of communication you want to have during the party. I asked Dave not to call me during the entire weekend because I knew I would be waiting by my phone, counting the seconds until I heard from him again.

- Plan something relaxing and fun with a friend or two during the party. I specifically didn't want to have our bachelor/ette parties at the same time because I didn't want either of us to be distracted by worry for one another. Still, treat yourself.

- Remember that the whole reason he's having a bachelor party is that he asked you to marry him—he'll be thinking about you the whole time. Well, okay, a good chunk of the time.

- If you have a close, trusted male friend on the trip, ask him to text you periodically to tell you everything's okay. Don't ask for details, just reassurance every so often.

And don't forget—you get to have your own bachelorette party, as well. For my party, fifteen girls came to a beach house in San Diego. It was just what I wanted: quality time with my girls, *sans* distractions. We spent each day hanging out and talking, and each night we made girly drinks, had a living room dance party, went out to a couple of bars and reflected—at the ripe old age of twenty-four—on our lost yet unlamented youth.

Dave wasn't nearly as worried about me as I was about him, but prior to my departure, he told me he wanted me to call him every night when I got home to tell him I was safe and sound.

Whatever you do for your bachelor and bachelorette parties, just make sure you have fun. Take the opportunity to reconnect with old friends, to introduce past VIPs to present VIPs in your life. And, yeah, you should probably wear a tiara.

SUSAN

As a romance writer, I believe in fairy tales. In particular, I believe in fairy godmothers. Elizabeth, an only child, has many of them. Through the years, my friends and those she made on her own have given her many spiritual gifts. Like the gorgeous, pastel-colored fairies in *Sleeping Beauty*, they gathered around, showering her with the gifts of kindness, empathy, wisdom, beauty...probably fashion sense from my friend, Carol.

Wedding time is a time to let the fairy godmothers back in. Invite the whole horde of them. You can never have enough well-wishers. Trust me on this. The bride has her chosen entourage—the wedding party. As the mother of the bride, you get to have one, too. Your girlfriends know how fun this is for you. Let them cheer you on! I spread the news like a computer virus, emailing photos and badly punctuated squeals around the globe. There's something about the announcement of a wedding that brings people's good cheer to the fore. I learned things about my friends' weddings I never knew before—the hilarity, the heartache, the surprises and the bombshells.

It's also a time to move closer to your daughter's friends. My own wedding was so tiny, I had only the maid of honor—my sister. Elizabeth kept adding beloved friend after beloved friend until the bridal party resembled a small army. I kept my mouth shut, however, because the nieces were in the picture, so I got my way. (Surprise.)

Now it was time to get to know the bride's friends. There was Molly, who is sweeter than your favourite Hallmark commercial. Lindsey and Aubrey, the fashionistas with hearts of pure gold. Funny, genuine Lucy...and Melissa, who once lobbied successfully to get me to name a character after her in one of my books.

These are the people who are going to be in your daughter's future. Cultivate them as friends, as people who will be there for her, through thick and thin. They're a lot like your own closest girlfriends—lovely, compassionate and always ready to listen to your troubles and triumphs.

There's something else you need to remember from *Sleeping Beauty*, though. That final pesky fairy, the one who put a curse on the poor kid and left in a whirlwind of fury, might be lurking in the wings. Unfortunately, you run into people like this, people who point out the percentage of marriages that fail, who warn you that planning a wedding will consume a year of your life and send you plummeting into debt—the doubting Thomasinas of the world. I refer to this sort of person as the turd in the punch bowl. (Again, sorry about that visual.) Tell yourself such people are put in the world to test your character—your reserves of patience, the depth of your wellspring of human kindness. And if that doesn't help, well...flush.

You needn't worry, though. A wedding tends to inspire people to be their happiest, most hopeful and kindest. Believe it, and it will be true.

CHEAT SHEET

TOO BUSY WARRING WITH YOUR MOTHER OVER WHETHER YOU SHOULD HAVE COUSIN BERTHA IN YOUR WEDDING PARTY? HERE'S YOUR CHEAT SHEET:

1. If you remember one thing after you put this book down, remember this: when people ask you who your bridesmaids are going to be—and they *will* ask you—smile and say you haven't thought that far ahead yet until you've made a final decision on your bridal party.

2. Find a gracious and special way of asking your bridesmaids (or bridesmen) to stand up there with you—even if it's just a nice card or a phone call on a Sunday morning.

3. Here's how guys ask: "Yo, you wanna be in my wedding?" "Sure, dude." "Cool. I'll look up the date and let you know...." That's not going to work for you.

4. If you're freaking out about who to include in your list of bridesmaids, don't split hairs over the number. Looking back on my wedding day, having a few more girls there did not affect my experience of the day—but regret from not having asked a dear friend would have lingered like the stench of cheap perfume.

7

ENTOURAGE

...all the people you need to be
the best bride you can be.
Wedding planners, photographers,
videographers, hairstylists

*Our wedding planners;
how we found them, how we
couldn't live without them.*

ELIZABETH

The average couple will spend 250 hours planning a wedding. Don't you wish I hadn't told you that? If it makes you want to race straight to Reno, hang in there. Help is on the way.

Four months after we were engaged, Dave and I quit our jobs, pulled up stakes and moved to Chicago so that we could start grad school. I know what you're thinking: "Wow, how amazing that you planned your whole wedding in the four months after Dave proposed to you!" Well, lemme get right to bursting your bubble: my wedding was barely a glimmer in my eye by the time I hopped onto the Amtrak Empire Builder (we rode the train to our new city because my fear of flying is such that horse tranquilizers barely take the edge off). In fact, here's the list of what we had accomplished as we pulled out of Union Station in Seattle:

1. Venue reserved
2. Menu theme chosen (although not yet battled-out with my mother)
3. Dress purchased
4. ...um, that's it.

See? If I had attempted to plan the rest of the wedding by myself, from fifteen hundred miles away, my head would have exploded. Dave and I quickly realized the vital importance of getting some foot soldiers on the ground, if you will, in Seattle. I wasn't about to lean on my local bridesmaids (I hadn't even officially asked them yet), and asking my mother was out of the question unless we were prepared to relinquish every last scrap of control we had over the wedding.

Yes, despite my pathological need to micromanage our Big Day (the apple doesn't fall far from the overbearing tree in the Wiggs household), I admitted that I was powerless over long-distance wedding planning and that my life had become unmanageable. I needed professional help.

Enter Good Taste Events. Even their company name inspired visions of an elegant, classic bride, sparkling from head to toe with happiness and grace. The home page of their website showed an unsteady-looking young man giving a toast to a newly married couple, with the caption, "Your wedding will be in good taste. The best man will be cut off early." With images of Dave's drunken cross-country team and their No-Shirts-Jägermeister-Circle-of-Death game flitting through my head, I called Good Taste and scheduled a meeting.

I mentioned "foot soldiers" a minute ago, but what we ended up finding was the Alexander the Great of wedding planners. Jody and her team deftly wrangled all our crazy ideas ("Breakfast for dinner? No problem. How do you feel about cardamom-scented French toast?"), consolidated eighteen versions of the guest list ("We noticed there are twelve different Susans invited. Do you want us to color-code them so you don't get them confused?") and dealt with our budding dramas ("The twins get into fistfights when they drink Pinot Grigio? We'll alert the waitstaff.")

And that was just the first meeting.

Throughout the wedding planning process, Jody and the Good Taste gals saved our lily-white hineys time and time again.

The first heroic rescue took place eight months before the wedding, when I received two save-the-dates for the weddings of college friends. Not only were their guest lists sure to overlap with mine by about twenty of my nearest and dearest, but they were both getting married within a month of Dave and me. As my arms broke out in hives and my throat began to constrict with panic, I called Jody and gurgled, "My friends are *stealing* my wedding guests! *Stealing* them! And now everyone's going to get those save-the-dates first, and realize they can't take *three* weekends off this summer, and they'll decide they can't come to my wedding because they hate me and I didn't send a save-the-date yet, and, and..."

"Shhh, honey," Jody said. "We're on it."

Two days later, everyone on our guest list found a silver envelope in their mailbox containing a custom magnet announcing our wedding date. Even better, Jody had managed to talk me off the ledge of wedding wars by reminding me that the friends who really love me would move heaven and earth to be there on my Big Day, wedding season or not.

A few months later, our modest 125-person guest list had ballooned up to a whopping 232 people (thanks, Mom) and we had outgrown our chosen venue, Court in the Square, in the heart of Seattle's historic Pioneer Square district. When we moved to Chicago, Dave and I were at least secure in the knowledge that our wedding would take place in the most unique, beautiful and affordable place we could imagine.

So you can imagine my reaction when we were told we had too many guests for a reception there. I wailed, I rubbed ashes into my scalp, I chewed my fingernails to the quick, I consumed eight gallons of Ben & Jerry's Cherry Garcia ice cream.

Shaking with fury and frustration (and more than a little annoyance at my mother for insisting that we invite her eyebrow waxer's entire extended family), I called Good Taste After telling me to sit with my head between my knees and breathe slowly into a paper bag, Jody and her team went into damage-control mode.

Within weeks, they had booked the Pan Pacific, a new and *very* swanky hotel in Seattle that was miraculously available for our wedding date. Even better, Jody had scoped out our original venue and engineered a seating arrangement that would allow us to keep our ceremony there. To that, I said, "I do."

And don't even get me started on the fires the wedding planners put out on the actual weekend of the event. A canceled rehearsal venue? No problem, let's rehearse the wedding in our favorite bar. A missing antique handkerchief for the ceremony? Here's a silk napkin that is even prettier. Another bridal party moving into the suite where we're supposed to be getting ready? Pfft—we're moving to a suite in Seattle's most famous hotel.

People, I won't lie to you: when I first got engaged, I envisioned myself planning the whole wedding without any help. I dreamed of calling my mom from rainbow-hued aisles of blooming flowers, asking whether she preferred anemones or mums and having her blithely reply, "Just get both, and make sure you order the most extravagant bouquets possible!" I pictured the shining faces of my various wedding vendors, always helpful and willing to take a wedding bullet for me. I imagined my mom watching *Father of the Bride* with me as we lovingly hand-addressed each invitation, pausing only to hold hands and talk about her own wedding to my dad twenty-eight years earlier.

I wouldn't even call that a pipe dream. It was an acid trip.

Sure, when I was first engaged, I was all gung ho. I even liked making guest list spreadsheets, for cripes sake. But the honeymoon (pun intended) was soon over. Before I knew it, I didn't want to think about signage and wedding favors and table linens. That's where the wedding planners came in—and, miraculously, they weren't faking it! They really *did* care about the minutiae that made me want to take a power drill to my temple.

Of course, the biggest hurdle was getting my mom onboard. As with most wedding-related expenses, this one wasn't small. To a woman who has managed to write two books a year; raise a daughter, an Airedale Terrier and a Doberman; have dinner on the table every night; and maintain a trim physique and good hair, the notion of hiring someone to make decisions for me set her head spinning. I had to show her that the wedding planners were so much more than decision makers. They would fight, tooth and nail, to make sure my loved ones and I would be able to relax and enjoy the fun.

This won't come as a surprise, but Jody is one of the few people I've known to rival my mother in her mastery of multitasking and efficiency. As soon as they met face-to-face, they did this grave little nod thing that said, "We're two of a kind, comrade." The deal was sealed when my mom saw Jody being kind to my slightly loopy grandfather, who only talks about denture glue and the price of bacon.

Now for the nitty-gritty—how wedding planners work. They usually charge a flat fee that covers a set range of services, such as helping you find your venue, suggesting and negotiating with vendors, creating a time line, keeping your wedding on budget and serving as the logistical point person in the days and weeks leading up to your wedding. We paid around $4,000 for Good Taste's services—a little lower than their usual rate because our budget was lower than average and we already had some of the bigger chunks figured out. But the cost of a wedding planner can cover the spectrum, based on the size of your event, where you're having it and what level of service you'll be getting. For $15,000, you can probably find a wedding planner who will give you a full-body massage on the morning of your Big Day. For $500, you might have a recent college grad who's eager to sink her teeth into event planning and is happy to keep things organized on the day of your wedding.

Early in our conversations with Good Taste, I asked Jody whether she thought it made sense for us to be spending 20 percent of our budget on our planners. I knew she would give me an honest answer—Good Taste doesn't do more than two weddings a month, and they would have no trouble finding another lucky couple to take our place if we couldn't afford their services. She wrote me a very kind email saying that she understood my concerns and that ultimately the decision was mine. "However," she went on, "keep in mind that part of our job is to keep you guys within your budget. More often than not, we end up saving our couples more money than we cost. We have relationships with wedding vendors in this area, and we can get discounts that simply aren't available to most people."

Dave and I sat down after the wedding to figure out how much money Jody and her team had saved us: the total came out to more than $5,000. The Good Taste gals knew how to pull some strings, that's for sure. In the months leading up to our wedding, they got rental fees waived, called in favors with industry connections and managed to find inexpensive alternatives for us that we never would have dreamt up on our own. In short: booya. Even Dave, the most frugal of frugals, agreed that Jody and her girls were the best thing that happened to our wedding (besides, you know, the two of us spending eternity together and everything).

SUSAN

Having conceived of and executed my own wedding in a thirty-minute, tequila-fueled frenzy one fateful day, I had no notion of what a wedding planner did. See, once Jay and I made up our minds to do the deed, we just wanted to get it done.

I was raised Catholic and although I had some major quibbles with the church (don't get me started), I did revere the pomp and ceremony of a Catholic wedding. I went to the local church and informed them that we wanted to be married in oh, say, the next month or so.

Who knew the church had Conditions? Since Jay had never set foot in a Catholic church, they wanted him to take marriage classes and show up for mass for six months running, keeping track of his attendance with personalized collection-plate envelopes to make sure he wasn't truant.

I said, "I'm pretty sure my fiancé is not going to do that. He doesn't want to be Catholic. He just wants to marry a Catholic girl."

The church played hardball. They expected to see him front and center, envelope in hand, for the next several months of Sundays.

"Would you consider officiating?" I ventured. "We could have it in a demilitarized—er, neutral—zone but it would mean the world to us if you'd officiate."

Nothing doing, said the padre.

"Well, maybe you could just be there, stand by us. My parents would love that."

Can't do it. No pay, no play.

"So how about you come to the reception? We're having cake and champagne—"

"What kind of champagne?" the padre asked. "Brut or dry?"

Thus ended my fleeting notion of a proper church wedding. I celebrated my new freedom with a bottle of the aforementioned tequila and a tome of Yellow Pages. There were several outfits listed under "Weddings," and I booked the first one to take my call. It was the Always and Forever Wedding Chapel. In the picture, it looked like something that belonged on the Vegas strip, complete with faux-Tudor styling, a cave-like interior and plastic flowers.

We signed up for a package that included an officiant, one variety of flowers (carnations dyed blue, if you must know), canned music and seating for up to twenty-five guests.

It was perfect. The more tequila I drank, the more perfect it seemed. "Let's go for it," I told Jay.

So when Elizabeth first came up with the idea of a wedding planner, I couldn't imagine what we would do with such a person, besides add her to the payroll. But, of course, in the beginning of it all, I couldn't imagine two venues, ten attendants, an unrelated torchlight parade causing a traffic jam to outer suburbia, squatters in the bridal suite, a raft of flower-shaped cupcakes and ten different hair trials.

Sound fun? Thought so. Here's my best advice—go ahead and hire the wedding planner if it's in your budget. You need one. Trust me on this. The right one will change this process from the nuptial equivalent of a root canal to a party you actually get to enjoy.

THE ONE-DAY PHENOMENON

If you're planning a wedding, you will be bombarded by the phrase *One Day*. It's an insidious little two-worder that is ultimately used to induce guilt or rationality (depending on whether you ask the user or her victim). One Day, as in, "How can you spend *that much money* on One Day?" or "It's just One Day...it doesn't matter if your best friend doesn't come!" or "You don't need a $12,000 Vera Wang dress that you're only going to wear for One Day." And it's always said in this somber, slow voice: "Calm down. It's just...One...Day." Sometimes One Day is accompanied by other zingers, usually budget-related, that force you to calculate awful figures, such as the cost of one hour of your wedding (a few thousand dollars, at least).

And, as a bride, your hands are pretty much tied. It's not as if you can say, "Nuh-UH, it's three-*hundred* days!" or "NO, I'm not actually spending tens of thousands of dollars on a five-hour event."

Well, I'm arming you now with your defense against the One Day–slingers—photography and videography. When someone insinuates that you should do your own hair because it will only last for One Day, you can say, "Actually, this day will be the most documented day of my life. I'll show these photos and videos to my grandchildren. I think it's only natural that I want to look my best."

See how I did that? Genius, right?

Unfortunately I figured this out a little late in the game, and spent the greater part of my wedding-planning journey torn between materialistic guilt and an overwhelming desire to spend my parents' life savings to make my One Day the best damn One Day anyone had ever seen.

Still, the nugget of truth in my One Day defense—*the most documented day of my life*—remains true for every bride. With that in mind, I set out to find the best people to follow me around and treat me like a celeb on my wedding day.

The wedding planner Elizabeth engaged first impressed me when she jumped in with her take-no-prisoners attitude and made this process a pleasure. She won our confidence from the start, and then during a last-minute flurry of RSVPs, she won my heart. There were a few requests for guests, and more guests...and guests of guests, twice removed... This was one of those last-straw moments, precipitating a prenuptial meltdown. And it was Jody to the rescue.

Did she rescue them by chasing the interlopers away with a flame-thrower?

No. She sent the bride a very simple email note: "Just welcome them with open arms and an open heart."

Vendors, venues and menus aside, this is the kind of perspective you want in a planner. One who is going to remind the bride not to freak out over a few extra bodies. A skilled, compassionate wedding planner understands how dangerously easy it is for the couple to fixate on minor details and lose the grand vision and the joy in what they're doing.

ELIZABETH

PHOTOGRAPHY

Your photographer and videographer will not only be hanging out near you for the most important moments of the day, but they will be creating the images you'll one day show to your kids and grandkids. Dave and I realized this and chose vendors whose style matched our vision. We didn't want some bossy, commandeering photobug who would wrestle my grandmother away from a conversation with a wedding guest and force her to pose on one foot, pretending to scarf down a cupcake. Nor did we want someone who liked to play with angles in their "wedding art" so much that my bridal portrait would end up looking like a cubist nightmare. I wanted a photographer and videographer who were *story-tellers,* who would find the special moments of the day and frame them in the most beautiful, real way possible. I wanted them to capture the sunbeam as it hit Dave's hair during the ceremony, to notice how beautiful my bridesmaids' shoes looked scattered on the side of the dance floor as they boogied their feet raw, to snap the moment my grandfather started crying as he gave our wedding toast.

Yvonne Wong, our photographer, fell into my lap fairly early in the wedding-planning process. I knew I wanted photos that were as much art as snapshots of the best day of my life. I would never hang a photo on the wall that looked like it was shot at a prom but with us wearing fancier clothes—you know, the pose where the couple faces out of the frame at a forty-five-degree angle, his hand stiffly on her hip, she with an uncomfortable, forced smile? Vomit.

I discovered Yvonne and her husband, David, on the blog that consumed my life for a good chunk of the engagement: WeddingBee. Go there at your own peril. Just make sure you don't have anything to do for the next week or so because you'll spend the whole time browsing through the message boards and blog entries by other brides-to-be like yourself. Anyway, during one of these marathon WeddingBee sessions, I saw some stunning engagement photos that played with light and shadow, focusing in on the details and capturing moments that many would overlook. Five minutes later, I had Yvonne on the phone and she passed my only other photographer test: she wasn't creepy. I mean, think about it. Your photographer is going to follow you around all day, and will likely be snapping photos of you as you bare it all and step into your gown. You know those classic photos of the woman's hands buttoning the back of the white dress? The bride was in the buff only moments before.

I'll let you marinate on that for a second.

See why it's so important to have a photographer who makes you feel comfortable?

I ended up needing Yvonne and David's coolness during the wedding reception, when I finally reached my breaking point with the posed photos. My face was starting to feel like it would crack, and I was trying to say goodbye to some guests who were leaving early, and for some reason I got a little misty-eyed (and not in a good way). Suddenly, Yvonne lowered her camera, pulled me aside, and said, "Go enjoy your party. I'll get candids of everyone who matters."

Prior to the wedding, she had asked me to fill out a form with the names of all the people I wanted to have in photographs. I also let her know that candid photographs were more important to me than posed images. After my little mini-meltdown, I went back to cutting an awkward rug on the dance floor (I'm the worst dancer of all time) and she sneaked around snapping photos of my loved ones.

I also opted to get a photo booth at our wedding. Unlike the tiny boxes found at carnivals, however, this photo booth was provided by our photographer and consisted of a white background, props and Yvonne's husband behind a professional camera. We stuck it in a corner by the bar and made sure everyone knew about it. Dear Readers, if you can have a photo booth, do it. I've seen some made with retro fabric backdrops and digital cameras on tripods. Something about a photo station makes guests go wild—and it ensures that your peeps will get in front of the lens if you end up skipping some of the formal portraits, as I did. The photos from our booth are some of my favorite from the wedding, and the consistent background gives them a uniformity that looks great when they're grouped together. And yes, I did think about how I would display my wedding photos before the actual event. You should, too.

Yvonne emailed me a teaser slideshow of the highlights from our wedding photos. Dave and I watched it while we were on our honeymoon, and we both shed a tear or two as we saw the first high-quality images of ourselves on what had been the happiest day of our lives. The show linked to our very own web page where we (and guests who had the address and password) were able to view all fourteen hundred

photos Yvonne and her husband and taken, and order prints. In addition, Dave and I received all our pictures on disc and in two thick books
of thumbnails for easy reference.

I won't lie: getting a professional album made can cost almost as
much as the photographer's time, so Dave and I promised each other
we'd save up and purchase a book for our first anniversary. (Of course,
then he got cold feet over the price, which has forced me to go rogue
and try to scheme up a way of buying the album without him knowing about it...but that's a story for another book called *How I Hid Your
Extravagant Purchases from Your Husband.*)

VIDEOGRAPHY

A family member told Dave and me that her only wedding regret was not
having a videographer there to record the ceremony and dancing at the reception. I'm so crazy about documenting special moments that Dave even
set up a video camera in the room where he surprised me with his proposal. So OBVIOUSLY I had to find the Best. Videographer. Of. All. Time.

Mitch of Cabfare Productions in Seattle is a man who has dated a
prize-winning female Elvis impersonator, has a mean golf swing and is
the proud owner of a 1970s-era video camera with a crack in the lens
(in addition to others, of course). He's a true artist—he weaves each couple's wedding video into a documentary, the plot of which is defined by
an interview he does with the pair. Most couples get interviewed after
the wedding, but since Dave and I were heading back to Chicago immediately after the honeymoon, we did ours ahead of time.

Mitch also offered Super 8 and high-definition video. In case you're
not wading through myriad websites and magazines about videography
yet, and thus don't know what Super 8 is, it's the grainy, cool-looking
film that most of us associate with old family movies. Think of the opening credits from *The Wonder Years.*

Most importantly, Mitch put Dave and me at ease from the moment we met him. He told us that our love inspired him, and that

documenting our marriage was going to be more fun than work for him. He personalized every single element of our wedding film and edited it in such a way that the final product was visually beautiful, entertaining, moving and complete.

Our wedding video ended up being perfect. When I watch it, I'm transported immediately back to the moment I said, "I do." Years from now, when I show it to our kids, they'll be able to experience our wedding as though they were sitting in the audience (which would admittedly suck for most kids—who likes seeing their parents be mushy?), but it's a testament to our classic, authentic wedding video.

Mitch was hands-down the best impulse decision I made about our wedding. I was lucky to find a talented, fun-to-work-with videographer, but if you end up not being able to afford a professional, set up a couple of cameras during the ceremony (if not other parts of your day, too) to capture the moment you become husband and wife. You'll be glad you did when you're able to watch the video more than a year later and remember exactly what you were thinking when you randomly let out a little giggle in the middle of your ceremony.

THE UPDO SAGA

I'm known for my hair. I never lost the blond ringlets that sprouted from my head when I was a tot, and I never quite abandoned the dream of having princess-hair on my wedding day. I didn't expect that this would be an issue because my style routine has always been blessedly simple: wrap in a towel, add a dab of mousse, air-dry...so imagine the possibilities given a professional stylist and two-plus hours in a salon.

Whenever anyone asked me what I was going to do with my locks on the wedding day, I would glibly answer, "Well, my hair is pretty easy to do so I'm going to deal with it later."

Big mistake.

The wedding goblins—you know, the ones who lie in wait, eagerly listening for the details about your wedding that you don't think merit much concern—pounced on my carefree attitude and served me up an epic trauma that I never saw coming.

Three months before my wedding, I embarked on a series of about ten different hair trials, each one a different ringlet of hell in Dante's *Inferno*. Every time I called a salon, I would specify my hair type and describe the style I was looking for. Each curt, aloof receptionist would promise that Tina, or Jessica, or Brett, or whatever stylist got me was an "expert" at that sort of thing. And every time I went to the salon, I would leave with my hair teased within an inch of its life, cast in a frizzy shell on top of my head like a cross between a helmet and a ratty wig. My shiny, bouncy curls would be reduced to dull, lifeless strands that hung like rattails out the back of a tangled nest on the back of my head.

You probably think I'm exaggerating.

I'm not.

Each time I had a trial updo, I would call Lindsey and Molly, my most trusted friends and bridesmaids, and ask them to critique. Lindsey would dutifully take photos while Molly attempted to find something positive to say about my newest hair nightmare—but even she, the Pollyanna in my life, couldn't make lemonade out of the lemons I kept ending up with. And Lindsey, the more blunt of the two, didn't bother sugarcoating the truth: "Do you think she's ever done anyone's hair before? Ever?" she said after a particularly bad trial that ended with me looking like a drowned Marie Antoinette.

I posted Lindsey's photos on my blog and my readers agreed—kindly, of course.

My mom, infuriatingly, found the whole thing hilarious. After the third bad updo, she cackled, "You look like George Washington!"

I had to be patient with her. She works from home, and sometimes goes weeks without being seen in public. So...her tact can be nonexistent from time to time. With the benefit of hindsight, I can see now that she was so lighthearted about it because she knew I would find the right stylist before the hair situation reached DEFCON 1 status.

A few weeks before the wedding, I had another hair trial at a posh salon in downtown Seattle. The receptionist who made the appointment assured me that this stylist was on the salon's "runway updo team" (whatever *that* meant) and had years of experience with weddings. I had high hopes. Surely someone who was on an actual *team* would be a pro at the type of wedding hair I wanted.

I came to the salon that day armed with a pile of photographs: one of Eva Longoria on the red carpet as an example of how I wanted my hair to look, and then a stack of the images Lindsey had taken after my previous trial disasters. "Here's what I *don't* want," I said firmly to the stylist. I went methodically through each of my other updos, pointing out exactly what I didn't like about each.

"In short," I concluded, having practiced my speech in the mirror before my appointment, "I want my hair to look exactly like this photo of Eva Longoria. I don't want it to look fuzzy, or ratty, or dull, or straight, or lifeless, or anything like these other pictures of me."

My stylist gave me a confident nod. "Don't worry," she said. "I can tell you've had amateurs working on you. I know exactly how to give you what you want."

I sighed, hoping she was right. I gazed down at the red carpet image resting in my lap. Eva's dark hair was a mass of loopy, soft ringlets that were pulled loosely off her face and back into a romantic mass of shiny curls at the nape of her neck. Her hair looked like mine, only more styled. It should have been easy to re-create this look with my blond locks.

So you can imagine my horror when this woman—a member of the "runway updo team," no less—began to tease my hair until the entirety of my skull was covered with a two-inch-thick mound of tangles. The ends of my curls struggled free of their teased roots, spiraling around my face like stringy Medusa snakes.

I should have said something at this point. But I have a deep-seated fear of confrontation (thanks, I'm sure, to the fact that I have no siblings and thus never learned how to fight). So I sat there in the chair, a growing sense of dread developing in my gut, trying to convince myself that the stylist did, in fact, know what she was doing and her vision would be revealed shortly.

Sadly, things got worse from there.

She pulled a couple of straggly, limp pieces of hair out around my face, straightened them with a flat iron, and let them hang in parallel lines down my forehead in front of my eyes. She pulled the rest of my teased, frizzy tresses back into a severe ponytail high on the crown of my head, then began braiding random strands. A few minutes later, she attacked the ponytail with a curling iron, crimping it randomly so the fuzzy curls poked out behind my head like a fountain of pure, unadulterated ugly. My ears—which have always stuck out the teeniest bit—seemed to spread from the sides of my face as though trying to take flight and escape the heinous mess that my stylist was creating.

"I'm going to give you something extra special," she commented as she raked a comb over the top of my head, causing the right and left sides of my hair to form large furry bumps at my temples.

She pulled out a Bedazzled white plastic daisy with a flourish. I was shocked. The flower's plastic stem was wrapped gaudily with lace and strands of cheap silver sequins. I didn't know an upscale salon like this would ever allow something so obscene within a two-mile radius of the premises. I watched in a near panic as she lowered the thing to the base of the ponytail she'd created and shoved it in. I could feel it scraping my scalp, a painful reminder of how difficult it would be to detangle my hair later that evening.

I managed a shaky smile, realizing there was nothing I could say or do to make this stylist good at doing hair. She was a lost cause. I tried to forget about the $80 price tag of this trial and set my sights on getting out of there as quickly as possible. Without letting her add any finishing touches to the monstrosity perched on my head, I exclaimed how pretty I looked, shook her hand and bolted for the door. I stopped long enough to pay for the trial and leave her a tip (she did *try*, after all, and I've never been a fan of stiffing service people on their tips).

As I slinked back to my car, hoping I wouldn't pass anyone I knew, my phone buzzed. It was Dave, calling to remind me that I was supposed to be at a cupcake tasting.

People, I had managed to keep myself together about the whole hair drama up until that point. I hadn't yet shed a tear over my bad updo trials, and I'd maintained a sense of humor about how ridiculously bad my hair had looked each time. I hadn't allowed myself to add up just how much money this bevy of appointments was costing me, and I refused to think about the number of hours I'd wasted squirming in the leather chairs of Seattle's salons. But this time I wasn't going to be able to go home, jump in the shower and erase all memory (other than a digital photo) of this horrific hairstyle. I had to go meet our wedding planners, Dave and our cupcake gal, with my hair looking like something pulled from a locker room shower drain.

I plunked myself down on a bench in the parking lot. I pulled out my phone, looked at the time and told myself I was allowed to flip out for five minutes. Then I had to go back to being a self-deprecating, upbeat bride who was completely confident in the belief that her wedding would go off without a hitch.

And then, friends, I had a five-minute sob-fest. This wasn't your normal, run-of-the-mill hiccupping cry. This was snot flying out of my nose in slimy projectiles that landed on the asphalt at my feet. Tears squirted in arcs from my eyes into my lap and drenched the ugly little pieces of hair the stylist had let hang in my face. I could feel my cheeks pulsing beet red as I struggled for breath, and my saliva got all thick and spitty the way a toddler's does when she's throwing a tantrum. My fingers curled into fists of rage, fingernails digging into the hot skin on the palms of my hands. Pit stains drenched through my shirt from my crying effort and I flapped my elbows wildly in a vain attempt to avoid getting body odor before my cupcake appointment.

It was epic.

And it lasted exactly five minutes.

Then I snorted my remaining snot back into my nose, dried my eyes, took a deep breath and forced myself to stop.

I arrived at my cupcake tasting appointment only a few minutes late, and though my eyes were still red and swollen, I knew nobody could tell just how intense my five-minute breakdown had been.

Heather, one of the Good Taste girls, was joining us for the appointment. When she saw my face, coupled with the disgusting pile of hair on my head, she immediately put her arm around me. "I have a friend who is *great* at updos," she said. "Trust me—she's done my hair before. I'll give her a call and we can stop this nonsense."

I won't lie to you; I didn't completely trust her. I'd been burned too many times before. But I meekly agreed to meet with Heather's friend and resolved to get through my cupcake tasting without any more fretting about my hair.

When I walked into the little room where we would be trying flavors, though, Dave was waiting for me. He knew me well enough to keep his trap shut about the cowpie on my head, but I could tell he was concerned by the obvious fact that I'd been crying.

"It's fine," I assured him. "Heather's got a plan."

And then I got to eat cupcakes, so I was a happy camper.

Later that afternoon, when Dave and I were both back at work, he IMed me. I could tell he'd been giving my hair trauma some thought, and I knew he genuinely wanted me to be happy with the way I looked on our wedding day. I also knew he didn't want me to be so done-up that he wouldn't recognize me at the end of the aisle. He started the conversation by talking to me about how great the cupcakes had been, how excited he was, yadda yadda yadda...and just as we were about to sign off, he said:

> **Dave:** by the way – i want your hair to be up or down for the wedding – none of this in between business
>
> **me:** hahaha okay
>
> **Dave:** i want it to look like my wiggs
> i really just love your hair
> and i love the way you look to me every single day

and i want you to look like my wiggs!

me: don't worry, i will

Dave: but it's been sticking out to the sides both times
i like it either dangling down or pressed in allllll the way
you can do whatever crazy pattern stuff to the back but from
the front it has to be *totally* pressed in!
you just have this beautiful face and it makes me smile and
bubble and feel waves of happiness

me: aw
don't worry
i don't want to look weird, either
i just want to be a more beautified version of my normal self

Dave: yes
it'll look JUST the same from the front...and howEVER you like in
the back!

me: haha okay

Dave: you can just show 'em your usual pull-up awesome sexy
gorge hair-do and then say, "i'm paying you to make this look
better in the back but the same in the front
...ready, set, go"

(For the record, that conversation is an unedited copy and paste
Isn't my hubby so cute, even on IM?)

I had to give the guy credit: he might not have known the correct
terminology to use when trying to talk about hairstyles, but he had a
point. My hair looked nice on a daily basis. I just had to find someone
who could add a little bit of va-va-voom to what I naturally had.

Heather set up an appointment with her friend, Jacquelynn, who
owned Sorella Salon just east of Seattle. Heather and Jacquelynn met
me in Sorella's cozy lobby, offered me a glass of iced tea and sat me
down to talk about my updo journey—the good, the bad and the frizzy.
I showed them photographs from my prior traumas, and they shook
their heads sympathetically.

"Well, you've come to the right place," said Jacquelynn.

From that moment on, I was in the hands of a true master. Jacquelynn smoothed my hair, brushing it out to a glossy sheen before taking a flat iron and constructing the shiny, loopy curls Eva Longoria wore in my inspiration photograph. While she and Heather entertained me with stories of other weddings they'd worked on together, she pinned my curls back, forming a soft pile at the nape of my neck and pulling a couple of pieces forward to frame my face.

Before I knew it, she unclipped the smock I was wearing to protect my clothes.

My hair...it was perfect. She'd taken the red carpet photograph I'd shown her and created a beautiful style that flattered my face like nothing I'd ever dreamed possible. It was, dare I say, *better* than Eva Longoria's hair.

Jacquelynn's next step solidified the burgeoning love I had for her: she offered to cut and color my hair a few weeks before the wedding to make sure that it was perfect for the updo on the wedding day. Then she armed me with two bottles of Bumble and bumble cream to make sure my hair was nourished and healthy. Realizing I had to look *gorge* at our rehearsal dinner the night before the wedding, I asked her to give me a blowout the evening before the Big Day.

A self-admitted control freak, Jacquelynn liked this idea. "Now I can make sure I know *everything* you have in your hair before I do your updo," she said. This was important because updos usually wear better with "day-old" hair that hasn't been washed immediately before styling. Obviously, this can get pretty annoying for stylists when their clients show up on the morning of their weddings with hair full of cheap, sticky gel.

The weekend of my wedding, I looked like a flippin' hair model. During the happy hour the evening before my nuptials, my hair was a glossy, golden sheet hanging down my back. On the wedding day...my hair was perfection.

CHEAT SHEET

WERE YOU TOO BUSY RECRUITING A CRACK TEAM OF PROFESSIONALS TO READ THE LAST CHAPTER? HERE'S YOUR CHEAT SHEET:

1. The right wedding planner can change your life. And bear in mind: more often than not, she'll end up paying for herself with the money you save.

2. Your photographer and videographer are going to be around you all the livelong day. Make sure you get good vibes from them in person as well as on film.

3. Know what you want and have inspiration photos for your hairstylist—and start looking early enough in case your search for the perfect beauty team turns into an epic saga, as mine did.

8

THE HYPE

Invitations and other printed matter

ELIZABETH

In the early days of the engagement, I was completely clueless about the world of invitations. Don't get me wrong; I'd seen *Platinum Weddings* on the WE TV channel and I knew some brides spent their IRA savings on platinum-plated, hand-embroidered invitations that had to be FedExed and weighed five pounds each. But I figured everyone else just went to the nearest FedEx office, ordered a bulk package of card stock, printed out single-sided postcard-sized invitations, slapped a stamp on 'em and called it a day.

Ohhh boy, was I in for a rude awakening.

Even my simple postcard idea, it turned out, could cost more than the couch I scrimped and saved for six months to buy. And don't even get me started on embossing, letterpressing, calligraphy, vellum and hand-stitching. My mom instilled in me a passion for all things paper-related, and for a girl whose favorite toy growing up was a sample folder from Paper Source, wedding invitations represented a box of candy. A stunning, expensive, delicious box of candy.

Certainly there was the frugal angel sitting on my shoulder, reminding me that most invitations end up in the trash, that nobody can tell the difference between 10 percent and 45 percent rag content, that going into debt over deckle edges and felt finishes was silly. I still agree with that angel, too—nothing in a wedding is worth going into debt over.

However, there was the other angel on my shoulder who reminded me that invitations were my opportunity to set the tone for the wedding. Sending guests a beautiful, thoughtful invitation was the first step in showing my gratitude for their support and willingness to be there for such an important moment in my life. I wanted each guest to know that we would be honored by his or her presence. A poorly thought-out invitation printed on scrap paper obviously wouldn't cut it.

And then there was the third angel in my life—the one I call Mommy—who had an entirely different idea for me. Still fixated on trying to get me to set my priorities on practicalities, my mother suggested that Dave and I send e-vites for our invitations. Yep. E-vites. When I reminded her that her own parents would probably be challenged, to say the least, by an email wedding invitation, she came up with this: "Well, send nice paper invitations to the old people who don't know how to use computers, and then e-vites to everyone else."

Right, Mom.

I knew there was a middle ground, an invitation that was nicer than a ~~spam message~~ mass email but not as extravagant as an engraved sterling silver plaque—but I had no clue what that invitation looked like. I ramped up for yet another slog through the impossible tangle of wedding information on the internet, but eight hours later all I knew was that DIY invitations would take me sixty-seven hours to complete and that the cost of stamps would increase by two cents less than a week after I planned on sending my invitations (meaning I had no room for delays). So, like any smart bride with limited time and a billion things to think about, I decided to pretend I didn't have to worry about invitations. Smart, huh?

A few weeks later, with my invitation worries carefully quarantined in a part of my brain, I got a phone call. My friend (and eventual bridesmaid) Aubrey was on the other end, and she was about to make me an offer I couldn't refuse: she had just started a letterpress company called Atlas & Campbell with her colleague, Tracy, and she wanted to design our invitations for us. The best part? She said her labor was a gift—all we had to pay for was materials.

Now, let's pause for a minute and have a little reality check. Most newly engaged gals don't have a close friend who just happened to start a letterpress company. I know that. But you'd be surprised how many connections you have that can help you out as you plan your wedding. That girlfriend who's an executive assistant? She orders flower arrangements for her office all the time and can hook you up with a local florist who's willing to give discounts to friends. Your brother who likes to woo the ladies with his emotional acoustic guitar playing? He can perform the musical interlude during your ceremony. Your fiancé's ex-girlfriend who started her own photography business? Not only can she be your photographer, but she'll feel so guilty over the way she dumped your man that she'll give you her services free of charge.

Just kidding about that last one. She'd probably intentionally take photos of you right when you've got a double chin.

Well, Aubrey was my clutch wedding connection. For the cost of postage, paper, ink and letterpress plates, Dave and I got one-of-a-kind, custom invitations complete with hand-stitching, vellum bellybands, and the rich texture left by a centuries-old printing machine. Here's the thing, though: paper is totally expensive. Even with free design labor and a friend who was trying her hardest to find me rock-bottom deals on materials, Dave and I were looking at spending upwards of a thousand bucks on our invitations.

That was 5 percent of our whole wedding budget.

With a heavy heart, I prepared to call Aubrey and tell her that I didn't think we were going to be able to afford her design services.

Dave saw me pouting as I picked up the phone and asked what was wrong. I burst into tears.

"We can't even afford PAPER for our wedding invitations! Do you hear me??! PAPER! We're going to have to send—" I snorfed a bubble of snot back into my nose "—e-viiiiiites!"

Dave looked at me like I had sprouted two heads. Enraged, I tried to force his understanding. "E-vites!" I screeched. "God! Nobody's going to come to our wedding because they'll be so offended that we sent... we sent...E-VITES!"

Like a practiced diva, I flounced dramatically into the bedroom, flung myself on the bed and commenced an unprintable wailing session.

Dave knew he had to follow me, or else.

Gingerly, he sat on the edge of the bed and patted my shoulder. "It's okay," he murmured.

"NO IT'S NOT!!!" I shrieked. "Do you *understand* what this *means*? It means that my mother...was...was...was RIGHT!" This thought brought a new feeling of hopelessness. I curled into a ball and stuffed the corner of my pillow into my mouth. (I've found this move to be very effective when you want people to think you're in need of serious attention and TLC.)

Dave was quiet for a moment.

I sneaked a peek at him from beneath my wet eyelashes. I recognized his expression as the same one he gets when he figures out how to build an IKEA shelf without any instructions—frustrated but enlightened.

I waited for him to speak.

"Actually..." he started slowly "...your mom may have been onto something."

"WHAT?! You can't be serious."

I looked at him with the eyes of a crazy person, ready to declare him a traitor who wasn't fit to be in my presence.

Dave looked thoughtful again. "What if we got people to RSVP online? We could still send the invitations that Aubrey designed, but we can get rid of those little envelope thingies [that's what he called the RSVP cards] and probably save on a ton of paper. And we're only inviting, what, seven older relatives who don't use computers? We can just call them."

Well, I hadn't seen *that* coming. But immediately I realized that my future husband had come up with a great idea. Having a paper-less RSVP system could dramatically reduce our costs. And, for karmic brownie points, it was eco-friendly.

I called Aubrey and told her Dave's idea. She was immediately onboard, and within the hour I had a revised invitation design. On the vellum insert that would be bound to the main body of the invitation, she added the line "Kindly reply by July 1 through our website, wiggsanddave.com."

The next day, I spent an hour building a form on our website (a search for "website form builder" returned a plethora of easy-to-use tools) that guests could fill out with the number of people in their party, the full names of everyone who would be attending (for place cards) and a little space for a message to us. When they clicked "Submit," their responses were sent to the email account that I had created especially for the wedding.

Done.

Our paperless RSVP system, combined with some killer deals Aubrey was able to snag from her paper supplier, cut our invitation costs in half. Nobody said a word about the missing RSVP cards. At least, not to my face.

And—What do you know?—my mom's original e-vite idea, while completely abhorrent to me, ended up being the inspiration for our eco- and wallet-friendly invitations.

Something tells me she wasn't surprised by that.

INVITATIONS: THE BRIDAL GATEWAY DRUG

All right, I'll admit it. I couldn't stop at just one fancy letterpress project. As with Franco Sarto mid-heel pumps, my first purchase merely opened the door for more. But this is where the real value of a dedicated designer comes into play. Aubrey and Tracy knew the exact fonts, styles and colors of our invitations and were able to create a whole wedding suite for us that coordinated with the original theme of our invitations.

When I called Aubrey in a panic ten days before the wedding, freaking out that I hadn't even started thinking about our wedding programs, she calmly told me she had it covered and created two hundred beautiful eight-page, hand-sewn booklets that featured all the readings from our ceremony, the names of our bridesmaids and groomsmen, directions to the reception venue and the names of our deceased relatives who we wanted to remember on our wedding day.

Then, five days before the wedding, I called Aubrey in hysterics, realizing I had completely forgotten to create place cards. This was a particular tragedy because not only had Dave and I spent hours assigning our guests to tables, we had spent the last nine months working on what I liked to call Project Place Card.

See, there's nothing I hate more than making small talk. At weddings, there are three questions you can always expect: "Where are you from?" "How do you know the bride or groom?" and "What do you do?" So I decided to save my guests from the hell of inane conversation by printing an interesting conversation starter on each of their place cards. We'd come up with 232 tidbits about our guests, hunting down details about our friends' dates and children whom we hadn't met by emailing and calling incessantly. The final list was incredible, and we'd learned more new and amazing things about our guests than we ever could have imagined. For example, my grandmother told me that my eighty-year-old great-uncle started "going with" my great-aunt when he was eleven years old. They were both coming to our wedding. My great-uncle's place card read, "Ask me about how I met my wife." For my college roommate who had an unfortunate (but memorable) incident involving a bottle of Baileys Irish Cream and a cell phone dropped in a toilet: "Ask me about flushing my Nokia." For my milky-skinned, blond friend who is 65 percent Cherokee, "Ask me about my tribe."

Awesome idea, right?

Feel free to steal it.

Leading up to the wedding, Dave and I scoured our memories for the most interesting details we could find about each of our guests.

When we weren't as close to some of the invitees, we asked our parents or mutual friends to fill in the blanks. It was a huge undertaking, but ultimately very rewarding.

Unfortunately, until five days before my wedding, I didn't realize that I actually needed to *create* these incredible place cards that had taken Dave and me months to plan.

Aubrey was all over it. When she arrived in Seattle forty-eight hours before the wedding, she handed me a box of personalized place cards that matched the rest of our wedding stationery perfectly.

Our entire suite of letterpressed wedding awesomeness included:

- Cocktail napkins
- Personalized book plates stuck inside the covers of our wedding favors, which were—surprise, surprise—autographed Susan Wiggs novels
- Wedding programs
- Invitations
- Place cards
- Thank-you notes
- Two different sizes of envelopes

I should note, for posterity, that my dear Aubrey added decorative hand-stitching on the invitations, thank-you notes, book plates and wedding programs. Now that's dedication.

CHEAT SHEET

CARESSING CREAMY PAPER SAMPLES INSTEAD OF READING? HERE'S YOUR CHEAT SHEET:

1. Work your connections. You've probably got a friend or two who can hook you up with some sweet deals for your Big Day.

2. Your invitation sets the tone for the rest of the wedding. See if you can find a simple way to personalize it and get your guests excited about coming.

3. Speaking of your guests, is there a way you can make each individual feel welcome and honored? Dave and I put a little personal detail on everyone's place card—and I'll bet you can top that. (Your choice of a mother-daughter wedding book *does* indicate a certain level of genius, after all.)

SAVE-THE-DATES

I'm not sure who came up with the idea of save-the-dates. You'll eventually begin to refer to your save-the-dates as STDs, which is appropriate since they share many qualities with their namesake: you never think they're going to happen to you, they keep cropping up at inopportune moments and they make you itch.

Still, since Emily Post tells us we must send our wedding invitations between eight and twelve weeks prior to the wedding, it's common courtesy to send a heads-up to guests a good six to eight months beforehand. Unlike our mothers' weddings, your own Big Day will probably require extensive travel and planning for a large number of your guests. STDs are your way of saying, "Hey, mark this on your calendar and start looking at airfare—I'll get back to you with the details later."

Early in our engagement, Dave saw a magnetic STD stuck to a friend's refrigerator. I wanted him to feel as involved as possible in our wedding planning process, so whenever he came up with an idea I pounced on it. One of the gals in our team of wedding planners is a talented artist, and she used a portrait of Dave and me to create an attractive, fridge-worthy, 3-by-5 magnet. To this day, I see our STD adorning the freezer doors in the homes of all our loved ones, and I give Dave cosmic brownie points for his ingenious magnet idea.

And don't think for a minute that I haven't made the "You've got my STD on your fridge!" joke about twenty times. Being married doesn't mean I'm any more mature.

9

RETAIL THERAPY

Creating your registry, bridal showers, and your once-in-a-lifetime opportunity to get the Lamborghini of espresso machines

ELIZABETH

Ah, the wedding registry. This was easily my favorite part of the wedding planning journey. Picture the scene: You think about your life with your husband, all the family dinners to come, the lazy Saturday mornings spent in bed, the swanky cocktail parties you'll host for your friends...and you pick out the objects that will populate those dreams. You drool over crystal candlesticks, paper-thin champagne flutes and espresso machines that mean you'll never have to leave your home for a good latte. You convince your frugal, practical soul mate that, yes, you do need sterling silver butter knives and you can't live without a $200 stainless steel Nambé candy bowl. So you make a list of all the things you want for your home. You put things on there that you would never dream of buying for yourself, because even though you just got a pay raise, you can't see your way to spending four hundred bucks on a down comforter. But then, magically, all the stuff you asked for starts showing up on your doorstep.

First, a note on having a registry at all: when we started to create ours, Dave hated the whole process. "It feels so acquisitiiiive," he would whine as I pawed like a nesting hamster through Egyptian cotton bath towels. After stopping to look up the meaning of the word "acquisitive," I sat him down and had a Big Talk. It went a little something like this:

"Yes, having a wedding registry takes the surprise and fun out of the gifts we receive. But our guests will be getting us gifts, whether we register or not, so would you rather have eight potato peelers, or one peeler and sheets for our bed? Our guests will prefer being able to select something from a list, too, instead of hoping we like what they've chosen. Plus, do you REMEMBER the Beanie Baby collection that Cousin Perdinella* gave us for Christmas?"

BAM! My little "We need a registry" speech worked like a charm.

Uncle Ben, Spider-Man's doomed father figure, said, "With great power comes great responsibility." Maybe he was talking about his nephew's newly acquired spidey sense, but he could just as well have said that to a new bride. You see, as a bride, you're now endowed with a mystical bridey power that attracts others to you, enticing them to throw you parties, compliment your figure and give you presents.

However, you won't hold onto this power for long if you take it for granted.

The wedding registry is the most tangible place you'll see this balance played out. As soon as you go live with your engagement— meaning that once you start to tell people about it—you're going to begin receiving gifts. And as soon as you get your first, ahem, lame present (matching his and hers toilet doilies, anyone?), you'll start your gift registry. Next thing you know, all the loot you picked out and put on your list will begin to arrive in giant, bubble-wrapping-filled packages. Sounds good, right? It's better than good—it's totally flippin' awesome!—until you mess up and forget to write a thank-you note. And, friends, nine out of ten of you will mess up.

I always fancied myself a great thank-you note writer. I went as far as prewriting my thank-you notes, leaving two lines blank for person- alization, before parties and job interviews. But I wasn't ready for the flood of unexpected gifts that arrived on my doorstep following the engagement party my mom threw for us.

Among the registry presents I received, there was a set of four place settings from my mom's friend, Venita, who also happened to be

* Names have been changed to protect the gifting-impaired.

the wife of my high school principal. Given her elevated status in my life, you'd think that I would have written a perfectly ruled, gushingly thankful note—especially considering that until we got her gift, Dave and I ate our meals off plastic plates. Additionally, we had just moved to Chicago and Venita was one of the few people to realize that it would be much more convenient for us if she sent our gift ahead to our new address so that we didn't have to move it across the country.

She was pretty much the best, most generous gifter we had come across yet.

And it's not like I didn't think about writing a thank-you note. Every week or so, I would realize that I still hadn't sent one and would mentally castigate myself for my rudeness...and then I would go make a bag of microwave popcorn and spend two hours watching *The Real Housewives of Orange County*.

Weeks passed. We used our new dishes every night, and slowly I began to forget that I had never thanked Venita for her generous gift.

One afternoon, my mom forwarded an email from Venita titled "Awkward question." Above the forwarded message, Mommy had written "SEND HER THANK YOU NOTE NOWWWWWWWWWWWWWW."

My stomach flipped. I could feel my cheeks flush hot, then go cold and tingly as I read the message Venita had written:

From: Venita

To: Susan

Subject: Awkward question

Dear Susan,

I hope you're doing well and enjoying the beautiful weather we've been having!

I'm writing because I have a somewhat awkward question to ask: Do you know if Elizabeth and Dave ever received the place settings I sent to them in Chicago? I tried contacting the company and they aren't able to tell me. I haven't heard from them and I'm worried the gifts never arrived!

We should get together for lunch again soon.

—Venita

I guiltily looked down at the beautiful white porcelain plate on the desk next to me, adorned with crumbs from the sandwich I'd made for lunch. I imagined that I could see the plate glaring accusingly at me. I felt like a thief—and in the wedding world, I *was*. See, you don't get your wedding gifts for free. Instead, you pay for them with gratitude, smiles and acknowledgment. Since these commodities don't cost you any money, you're pretty much a bad person if you neglect to fork over the goods.

I spent the next hour crafting my reply, forcing Dave and my mother to edit and reedit multiple drafts.

From: Elizabeth

To: Venita

Subject: A thank you and an apology

Hi Venita!

I owe you a huge apology (and thank you at the same time!)— my mom mentioned that you hadn't heard whether we received your gift from Oneida, and to my dismay I realized that Dave and I completely overlooked writing you a thank-you note. Moving to Chicago turned our lives upside down, and I'm very sorry to say that my etiquette skills are one of the items I'm still unpacking. The dinner sets are absolutely incredible and not a day goes by that we don't use them and LOVE them. They're actually the first real plates we've owned!

I hope you'll accept my sincerest apologies for not letting you know that your gift was received and greatly, greatly appreciated.

Aside from forgetting our manners, Dave and I have been doing very well in Chicago. So far, we're surviving the cold and what the city lacks in good weather it makes up for in a wonderful culture! Of course, we miss our families, but it's been fun to make a new life for ourselves in this incredible place.

Again, I'm so sorry that I forgot to thank you and your husband. Your gift truly helped us make a home for ourselves out here in Chicago—otherwise we'd still be eating off disposable plates and drinking our tea from mugs I bought at the Salvation Army!

Thank you once more.

Best,

Elizabeth

As soon as the email was sent, I scrambled to hand-write a thank-you note as well. That's the other thing about thanking people for the gifts you receive: go hand-written or go home. I went rogue and sent an email in the Venita situation because it was more important to let her know as soon as possible that I'd gotten her gift, but I wasn't about to gyp her out of the one thing she could expect in return for her generosity.

Dear Venita,

Thank you once more for the incredible place settings you sent. They really have made our condo feel more like a home here in Chicago—no more disposable dinnerware for us! You were so kind to send the settings to our new address. Apologies for the delayed note, and thanks again!

Best,

Elizabeth & Dave

I haven't been late on a thank-you note since. In fact, Dave and I instituted a rule after the whole embarrassing situation with Venita: no using the new gift until we write a thank-you note for it. After the honeymoon, when we came home to a mountain of boxes, we wrote our notes as we opened each package. I suggest you do the same, or endure the epic, traumatic guilt you will experience when your generous friends have to ask about the gift they sent you when they never heard whether you received it.

SHOWERED IN LOVE

Ah, the bridal shower. Dreaded by some, eagerly anticipated by others, it can be one of the more polarizing experiences of the wedding planning process. I was one of those brides who couldn't WAIT for my bridal shower—I was excited for the ribbon bouquet, the wrapping paper dress, the themed menus. The wedding gods must have known this, because I had not one, but two bridal showers thrown for me. The first was a surprise shower put on by Dave's mom at her home in Vancouver, Canada. She lured me there with a story about celebrating Dave's birthday as a family, but when I walked in the door, I was greeted by a roomful of Dave's female relatives, two of my bridesmaids, my mom and an opera-singing chef named Pepe.

The theme of the shower was cooking and baking, and as Pepe sang and taught us how to prepare a beautiful Italian meal, I unwrapped gorgeous copper pans and glass nesting bowls.

I have a theory about why many women dread their own bridal showers: first, it's a little bit awkward to sit in a roomful of people as they watch you open gifts. Sure, it was fun when you turned seven at Chuck E. Cheese's, but we're adults now and have become accustomed to receiving most gifts in the mail after they've been purchased online by our other adult friends. Second, and worse, your bridal shower is likely thrown by your mother or future mother-in-law—meaning that you won't know every single person there. So, ultimately, you're sitting in a circle of people, many of whom you don't know, opening a pile of gifts they've given you and trying to act grateful when you're not even entirely sure which one is Bitsy from your mom's aerobics class and which one is Delilah from her book club.

Well, I developed a little trick for faking it through a party where you probably won't know everyone's name: first, you sloooowly open the attached card, keeping a discreet eye out for anyone whispering, "This one's from me!" to her neighbor. Then, look at the name at the bottom of the card. Keeping your eyes on the card, say, "What a gorgeous note, Drusilla!" Now this is the crucial moment. Pretend you're still reading the rest of the note she wrote, when in reality you're waiting for Drusilla to respond to your compliment. BINGO! As soon as she says, "You're welcome," or "Oh, dear, I found that at the Dollar Store," look up and smile at her, then rip into the wrapping paper.

One potential mishap: If Drusilla is too busy sucking down her mimosa, she might not respond to your comment about her card. In these rare cases, look around dazedly at the circle of women and say, "Now where's Drusilla? I don't see her..." and when she waves or someone points her out to you, say, "Ah! I thought you were on the other side of the room!"

Of course, knowing this method, you could save yourself a lot of anxiety by asking the host of your shower to discreetly nod in the direction of each gift-giver as you read her name from the card. Or you could ask your hostess to provide nametags or play some sort of name game with your guests, but you should make sure you've got a backup plan in the event that your menopausal hostess's house is colder than a meat locker and all the guests put on cardigans that cover their "Hi, My name is..." badges.

And if all else fails, force yourself to tear up. They'll forgive you for anything if you play the part of the emotional bride well.

SUSAN

Don't get me started on bridal shower etiquette. I made the mistake of consulting some wedding books, reading the rules and regs of giving and receiving until my eyes glazed over. And then I did it my way. Well, my and Sheila's way, to be honest. Sheila is the go-to BFF we all need in our lives, the one with the big smile, the big laugh and the can-do attitude. We put our heads together and planned the silliest bridal shower our fevered minds could conjure up.

We kept it simple, ensuring that no one's eyes would glaze over. The invited guests—women I've known and loved for years—received an email invitation, with the time (a flawlessly sunny Pacific Northwest summer afternoon), the place (my patio), links to the gift registry and a promise to award a prize to the most creatively wrapped parcel. And then we called a caterer. We're nutty, but not stupid. Nobody wants to run around cutting cucumbers into little flower shapes when we could be sitting on the patio, sipping a kir royale. Or better yet—the signature cocktail Sheila named especially for the event: The Pink Wiggs. Get a jar of hibiscus flowers in syrup (yes, these do exist), place a flower in a champagne flute and cover it with your favorite bubbly. Done!

The gang showed up in force, we played games, we ate and drank, we oohed and aahed over presents. At the very end, Canadian Dave showed up and I paraded him around like a Great Dane at the Westminster Dog Show, to wild applause. By this point, he was resigned to the idea of being my son-in-law, and all that entails.

As for me, what on earth did I want to give my daughter as a wedding gift? A place setting that looks like the other eleven place settings she signed up for? Couch pillows or a fancy duvet cover? A kitchen appliance? Sorry, no.

I'm a big believer in letting the universe hand you what you need. When it comes to picking out the perfect gift to give your daughter on the occasion of her wedding, it behooves you to pay attention to the world around you. As the bride's parents, you want to give them a grand gift. Something memorable and personal. Something they'll treasure all their lives. You want to give them something that celebrates who they are and all your hopes and dreams for them...but at the same time, doesn't burden them with an object that's going to be a pain as they cart it with them, albatross-like, through life. So what, after childhood, graduations, all those holidays and birthdays, is left to give her?

That's where the universe comes in. Pay attention, and all will be revealed, right?

In my family, there is an epic platter that is given to each woman on the occasion of her twenty-fifth wedding anniversary. We have a theory that this is because it takes twenty-five years to find someone willing to take on the silver filigree and crystal monstrosity. It's exactly the sort of thing you don't want around. Five minutes in the open air, and the thing is tarnished. It's also fragile, and so it spends its life swaddled in bubble wrap, taking up space.

Clearly, there was one thing I knew I'd *never* give—a fragile anniversary platter of any sort. Seriously, no one needs such a thing, particularly a pair of newlyweds who will, according to statistics, move an average of four times before they buy their first home.

Unfortunately, as you've probably already guessed, the universe had another plan. Jay and I decided that, in honor of her wedding, our adored and only daughter was going to receive (wait for it) a *platter.*

I *know,* right? But I don't make the rules. I met artist Sally Mara Sturman in another context entirely, but when I saw her work, I was a goner and in-stantly commissioned a ceramic platter from her. Sally's art is whimsical, personal, colorful and a perfect way to capture the joy of the occasion.

The universe gave me Sally, and I had to give Sally some idea of what to depict on the platter. Happily, she had visited our home and Seattle, so she was already familiar with the ferryboats, the mountains and Puget Sound, the gulls and eagles. In her inimitable, charming style, she created a panorama of these iconic images, with a small vignette of a couple sailing off into the sunset, toward a shining happily-ever-after. Every detail in the picture had meaning to the couple, from the name on the stern of the boat to the tiny depiction of Barkis the dog, paw raised in salute from the shore. On the back, she recorded the date and a personal message. Years from now, I hope they'll use it to serve canapés or birthday cake or even a pizza pie to their friends and family.

Is it fragile? Sure it is, just like a marriage. This simply means is they're going to have to work extra hard in order to make sure it doesn't break.

CHEAT SHEET

DID YOUR NEW CHINA PATTERN OBSESSION DISTRACT YOU FROM THIS CHAPTER? HERE'S YOUR CHEAT SHEET:

1. Go ahead—register. Otherwise, you'll end up with a matching set of crocheted toilet doilies and seventeen toasters.

2. Go high-end. If you want that absurdly expensive grapefruit knife, put it on your list. And if nobody ends up getting it for you, lots of stores will give you the option of purchasing it at a discount.

3. Write your thank-you notes NOW. As soon as you get a gift.

10

JUGGLING ACT

Taking the guesswork out of guests

ELIZABETH

Brides, you know how excited and sparkly you feel right now? You're probably over-the-moon at the prospect of *anything* wedding-related because, if you're anything like me, you played the "when we're engaged" game with yourself for at least a couple of months (okay, years) before your honey proposed to you. So here's my advice: use that energy immediately. Do some of the nitpicky stuff now, while it still seems fun to you.

For example, make the guest list before you're all wedding-ed out and you want to stab yourself in the eye with a dull butter knife whenever you think about it. Dave and I spent the first morning after we were engaged brainstorming all the people we wanted to have at our wedding. Later that week, we created an Excel file titled "Everyone Who's Anyone–Wiggs-n-Dave's Totally Awesome Guest List." (Note: I highly recommend going overboard in the "Wedding!!!!!!" file you've probably just started on your computer. All our documents and spreadsheets had bodacious names, and as I grew more and more weary of dealing with the brass tacks of the wedding, those titles gave me a reason to smile and remember how excited I was about the whole process.)

If you're such a saint that the idea of jay walking makes your unsullied-by-worldly-things skin crawl, skip this next part. We're about to get a little dicey.

I know what you're thinking: "But I don't have *time* to make our guest list yet! I might be engaged, but I still have a fifty-hour-a-week job, and a social life, and four episodes of *Gossip Girl* on my TiVo!"

Well, brides, I'll share a little secret with ya. And I feel comfortable doing this, because any woman who has ever planned her wedding while holding down a full-time job will back me up. *Wedding planning can look just like work.* You know that spreadsheet your manager asked you to create to illustrate your firm's operations budget allocation for the past six months? Be honest: you've been putting it off because it's boring, even though you know it will only take you ten minutes once you get started. Well, do the flippin' budget allocation. Now. And when it's done, don't say a word to anyone in your office. Open a second Excel file and start your guest list. When your manager stops by and asks how the budget spreadsheet is coming along, squint at your Aunt Matilda's mailing address and say, "You know, I hit a couple of bumps with it, but I'll get it to you by the end of today."

Booya. Your guest list is coming together, your boss thinks you're working your tail off and you're actually already done with your boring project.

Is it ethical? No. Does every working bride do it? You bet.

Let's be honest with each other here: chances are, you're not working 'round the clock while you're in the office. You're playing Sudoku, emailing your girlfriends about the cute new shoes you just bought, refreshing the Nordstrom home page to see if that pair of True Religion jeans finally went on sale.

So (and let's turn off our moral compasses here) you're not *really* being unethical. You're just replacing your old forms of procrastination with a new one: wedding planning. And, bonus, your wedding is probably all you can think about right now so you'll be giving yourself an outlet for your obsession that will allow you to focus more fully on your job when you need to. Yeah...right. Planning your wedding at work will actually make you a *better* employee. Yep. Just keep telling yourself that.

I did.

And the gal who sat next to me in the office—the one who had just gotten married a couple of months ago—kept giving me a knowing wink whenever I started to look abnormally captivated by the data compilation I'd just been assigned.

Just make sure you don't miss any deadlines.

THE GUEST LIST—OR, THE ONLY TIME
YOU'LL EVER HAVE TO RANK YOUR FRIENDS
IN ORDER OF THEIR IMPORTANCE TO YOU

The wedding isn't all about you. I mean, yeah, you're the one in the big white dress, and sure, everyone keeps reminding you that it's "your day." But, look, it's also a very important and moving day for your parents. After all, no matter what sort of relationship you have with your family now, you were once a little baby girl they never dreamed would be a wife. For your mom or dad, it's like seeing that younger cousin who lives in Saskatchewan for the first time in ten years ("holy smokes, she's tall...and old"), except a gazillion times more intense. Keep that in mind when you're building your guest list. They might need some of their peeps around for support. If your venue has a strict limit on the number of people you can have, give your folks a concrete number of guests they're allowed to invite. Don't be stingy with them, either—especially if they're paying for the wedding.

You want Mom and Dad to be comfortable and happy and not feel like they're stuck at a college party. Our final guest list of 185 people (the rest of our 232 invited guests couldn't make it) included 55 of my parents' friends. So, yeah, maybe the Wiggses went a little overboard. I can say that with complete confidence now, after seeing the shoe-sized hole in the tulle underskirt of my dress, courtesy of my mom's inebriated, close-talking friend. But it was better than having my parents feeling like they just paid through the nose to hang out with a bunch of krumping twenty-five-year-olds.

A good rule of thumb is to give each set of parents at least 10 percent of the head count. And no, this percentage does not include relatives you would invite anyway. Let your parents choose their people after you and your fiancé have formed your own guest list—that way you can't screw them over by claiming that your sister counts as one of your mom's guests. Think about it: for a 150-person wedding, your mom and dad get fifteen people they don't have to clear with you. Fifteen people who will make your folks feel more at ease and special on their baby's wedding day. Same goes for your in-laws. You and your fiancé, on the other hand, will still have a full 120 spots, and that's not so shabby. Particularly if you're not footing your own bill.

Another note: never invite someone thinking, "They'll *never* come." Those are always the people who show up with their unmedicated kids, a Jack Russell terrier with abandonment issues and your ex-boyfriend, whom they happen to know through their halitosis specialist. My mom convinced me to invite a ton of people this way. When I protested that we were already at capacity, and that additional guests would suck up the pennies left in our budget, she would say, "Just invite them—people hate coming to weddings. They'll send you a gift and never actually show up."

As you probably figured, many of these assumed no-shows not only ended up coming to the wedding but also were among the most demanding guests. Then again, I can say with absolute confidence that my wedding day was the happiest day of my life, and I wouldn't want to toy with myself by wishing things could have been different. Maybe I would have had a worse time if my mom's half-insane motivational speaker friend hadn't shown up, gotten way too drunk and passed out in a chair next to the crepe station.

So if and when your mom's zany acquaintance descends upon your wedding—when she brings your ex-boyfriend as her "plus one," despite being thirty years his senior...and when your fortieth cousin thrice removed comes and brings all four of his teenaged daughters and their greasy, emo boyfriends...and when a crowd of your nemeses from high school hears about your wedding from guests on the ferry on the way over and pretends that stopping by the reception to "say hi" and steal some cupcakes isn't the same as crashing your wedding... you'll just have to smile. Because, yes, this is the happiest day of your life, even when things go wrong. And all the people who show up— even the ex-boyfriend who's glowering at your new husband from the corner of the room—are supporting your union just by being there. You're celebrating the start of your married life, and everyone present will bear witness to that, adding their energy and spirit to fuel the joy you're experiencing.

And bonus—you now have a spouse who will happily join you in talking major trash about the schmoes who executed epic wedding faux pas. Faux pases? Whatever.

FOOD, GLORIOUS FOOD: DEVELOPING YOUR MENU AND CHOOSING YOUR DESSERT

Remember, back in the chapter on budget, when I talked about making a list of wedding priorities? Dave and I made a list of all the elements we wanted in our celebration and then listed our priorities from most to least important. Stuff at the top of the list got lots of money; stuff at the bottom, if it ended up in the wedding at all, was as cheap as we could make it.

For us, menu was near the bottom. At one point, I considered putting boxes of Honey Nut Cheerios and pitchers of milk on the tables and calling it a day. Considering all the weddings I've ever attended, the only food I can remember is the clam linguini that gave me food poisoning.

I feel bad saying so, because I have vivid memories of my girl-friends agonizing over whether they should serve filet mignon with the lemon beurre blanc sauce or the red wine peppercorn reduction. I had a friend who nearly canceled her wedding over sourdough rolls.

And don't even get me started on the cake dramas.

So when I sat down over brunch with my mom to talk about the menu for our wedding, I really couldn't have cared less what we ended up serving. If my guests were anything like me (a decent possibility since most of them were either friends or relatives), they would only remember the food if they ended up seeing it a second time as it arced from their mouths to the porcelain god in the bathroom. Seriously— think back to the weddings you've been to: do you remember what you ate? Can you get any more specific than what type of animal was on your plate?

I'd done enough research to know that catering could cost me the equivalent of a one-bedroom condo with a balcony and stainless steel appliances in New York City. No T-bone steak and lobster tail for me. Still, I wanted to make sure that I didn't serve anything so lame (Spam and Miracle Whip sandwiches?) that my guests would walk out.

My mom and I were seated in one of Seattle's most famous brunch spots as we started tossing out ideas for the menu. I wasn't exactly inspired by anything we came up with, though. Chicken breast? Too dry and boring. Salmon? The taste makes me gag, so, uh, no. Halibut? Too expensive. Duck? Ever read *Make Way for Ducklings?* No way was I gonna eat something that had once been a fuzzy yellow ball of adorable.

I looked down at the giant brunch menu our waiter had just plopped on the table and, as usual, couldn't make a decision about what to order because it all just seemed so *yummy.* God, breakfast food is good.

"I wish I could just have *this* be the menu for our wedding," I muttered.

And then sucked in my breath.

"What's wrong?" my mom asked, looking at me cross-eyed from behind her 85 times magnification menu-reading glasses. She leaned in conspiratorially. "DO YOU NEED A TAMPON?" she whispered loudly, "BECAUSE I DON'T HAVE ONE ON ME."

"Ugh, Mom! No!" I said, swiveling my head to see if any of our fellow brunchgoers had heard. "But I just realized...*everybody* loves brunch. Why don't we just forget about fancy food and serve breakfast for dinner?"

I looked at her expectantly, waiting for the "Ah-ha! My daughter is a genius!" moment.

She took off her glasses and blinked owlishly at me.

"Breakfast...for dinner?" she said slowly. "But...that's so *weird*."

"No, it's not!" I insisted. "Think about it—we can have an omelet bar, and serve crepes, and fruit, and bacon—I mean, who doesn't love bacon?—and...and...we can have a French toast mountain instead of a cake!!!"

I looked down at the menu in my hands and another thought hit me, one that I was sure would send my mother into paroxysms of gratitude and happiness.

"AND—breakfast food is cheap! We won't be serving meat for the main course, so just think—it can't cost more than fifteen or twenty bucks a head!"

My mother looked at me blankly.

I didn't care. In my mind, the matter was settled. I knew Dave, the box-and-a-half-a-day cereal eater, would love the idea. That afternoon, when I told him about my stroke of brilliance, the look of adoration he gave me let me know I was right. We would serve breakfast for dinner, have French toast instead of cake, and my mom would have to deal.

OH. CUPCAKES.

Yeah, we were planning to have a pile o' French toast for dessert, but as soon as my mother realized that this crazy idea was actually going to happen, she called me up and told me that cake was "required." Apparently, one of her friends had thrown a hissy fit about it and she bowed to peer pressure. Then, HORROR, she decided that not only was cake required, but we had to serve cupcakes—the one wedding dessert that made my stomach turn in disgust.

Cupcake towers just don't do it for me. They're inelegant, busy and generally childish. But up till that point, my mom's input for the wedding had been largely restrictive: you can't have that many guests, you can't have nice invitations, you can't have six bridesmaids. I was determined to say yes to the one positive command my mother had issued.

So I started researching. And I realized that cupcakes don't *have* to be tacky. I could serve cupcakes, keep my mom happy and stay true to my modern vintage style. Forget cartoony cupcake towers splashed with all the colors in the Crayola box; there were cupcake bakers who could create elegant, subtle arrangements in an array of mouthwatering flavors that would have guests begging for more.

My wedding planners caught wind of the idea and sent me a flurry of photographs from past weddings featuring—even better—*mini* cupcakes! Each little cake was two bites of moist, flavorful goodness and the caterers didn't go around the dining room afterward throwing away the dry bottoms of large cupcakes that guests discarded after making themselves queasy from eating the icing first.

And lucky me—Seattle was quickly becoming a cupcake capital. People in the Emerald City had taken notice of the powers of the cupcake, and sweet little independent shops were popping up all over the place with vintage signs and inspiring names like Cupcake Royale, Trophy Cupcakes, the Yellow Leaf Cupcake Company and—with an evil cupcake as their logo—Look Cupcake. Being an evil cupcake myself, I was instantly sold on Look. But their logo was only the beginning of the awesomeness. Look Cupcake was the only cupcake company in Seattle to offer "filled" cupcakes—in other words, not only was there delicious buttercream icing adorning the dome of the cakes, but the bakers had piped filling into the center of each in flavors like mojito cheesecake, salted caramel and chocolate ganache.

I sat down with the owner of Look Cupcake, Rhienn Davis, and immediately knew I had met my cakey match. She plopped her laptop on the table in front of me, apologizing for the missing "L" key that her two-year-old had pulled off and the sticky, sweet-smelling mousepad.

Unlike so many other people in the wedding industry, Rhienn was real. She wasn't a manicured robot, ready to hit the "Play" button on her sales pitch and convince me to spend four times my budget on her product. She had darling children, a husband and a young business of her own, and she knew that what I wanted was an easy, delicious dessert that didn't put me in the poorhouse.

We decided on four cupcake flavors, and there was no *way* I was going to pass up on her incredible taste options. My mom's bland suggestions of chocolate and vanilla cupcakes flew out the window as I made my selections: The Feather Boa (coconut cream cake, mojito cheesecake filling, vanilla Swiss meringue buttercream), Summer in Your Hand (lemon cake with raspberry cheesecake filling and raspberry meringue buttercream), a vegan Emperor's New Grove (vegan chocolate cake, Valencia orange vegan ganache and Valencia orange vegan buttercream) and, the pièce de résistance, a combo that I came up with myself, a custom chai cake with salted caramel filling and hazelnut meringue buttercream. It's now called The Wiggs. Sometimes my own awesomeness frightens me.

Everything was going swimmingly, until I called my mom two months before the wedding to share the good news that her cupcake dream would come true. See, she thought that not only would cupcakes be the perfect alternative to cake, they would be less expensive than a four-foot, tiered monstrosity. But since we were getting minis and had an array of flavors for our guests to sample, we were going to need three cupcakes per guest, or, with our ballpark two-hundred-person wedding, six hundred cupcakes.

When my mom heard that, a blood vessel burst in her eyeball.

"Six...*hundred* cupcakes?" she gasped. "No. No no no nononononono. Forget it! Look, just go to a cupcake store the morning of your wedding, get three dozen cupcakes, and call it a day. You don't need six hundred cupcakes. Most people won't even touch your dessert!"

Funny, wasn't that the exact opposite of her argument in which she informed me that I was "required" to serve cake, since cake was the "one thing that wedding guests want"?

And she forgot the fact that this close to the wedding, I was a veritable expert on serving sizes and the eating habits of wedding guests, and I knew that if we were going to serve cupcakes, we were going to need a lot of them. As my mom's voice grew louder and more panicked on the other end of the phone, I interrupted her. "Mommy, I'm sorry, but you wanted cupcakes, and we're going to have them. And we're going to do it right." I slowly lowered the receiver and hit the "End" button. This time, I knew, I was correct and I would simply have to do it without my mother's go-ahead.

On the day of the wedding, we ended up having a snafu with the hors d'oeuvres and they didn't get served during the cocktail hour while Dave and I were getting our portraits taken. So, like starving wildebeests, my guests stormed the cupcake display, which was tucked away for later, and devoured the entire thing. A plate of only eight cupcakes survived unscathed, and our apologetic wedding planners whisked them away to the bridal suite so Dave and I could enjoy our own dessert. I never did end up finding out who ate the first cupcake and tipped off the rest of the guests that it was okay to plunge into my carefully arranged dessert table. And if I do...well...let's just say that he or she owes me a blood debt.

In the end, six hundred cupcakes was the right number. I think my mom ended up realizing that her objections to the cupcake volume had more to do with nerves over the impending event than some deep-seated psychological paranoia related to confectionary treats. And I definitely caught her shoveling a whole mini cupcake into each cheek when she thought no one was looking. I may have been caught up in my wedding day, but don't think I wasn't watching my mommy to make sure she was enjoying it every bit as much as I was.

SUSAN

Okay, so I kept it zipped all through the bacon-and-eggs menu, the save-the-planet no-flower rule, the cross-town commute between venues...but...no *cake*? C'mon. No cake? What? How can it be a wedding with no cake?

Sigh. In my almost-not-a-wedding a hundred years ago, the cake was just about the only traditional element we had. Maybe that's why it just felt wrong to flop a pile of French toast in a chafing dish and call it dessert.

Deep, cleansing breath. And then clarity: there will be cake. There *must* be cake. How hard can it be? You don't need a Taj Mahal made of sugar dough, just a sweet, unassuming little dessert so the guests will all know beyond doubt that they've been to a wedding.

Simple, right?

Something had to be done.

I came up with a compromise—cupcakes! They're adorable. Everybody loves them. They cost about $20 per dozen. Now, that seemed a little pricey to me, but figuring one cupcake per guest, it works out to a couple hundred bucks, right?

Right?

And they're easy. A no-brainer. What's simpler than platters of cupcakes, artfully arranged on a table? And they won't add to anyone's work load either, because how hard can it be? You tell the cupcake-maker you want a few dozen in chocolate, vanilla and strawberry. No nuts; people get sued over nuts these days. Just three flavors with that nice little swirl of icing on top. Maybe some sprinkles, and we're good to go.

Right?

Ohferpetesake. You're way ahead of me, aren't you?

She spent hours researching cupcakes.

Who could have imagined that she—your erstwhile sane, practical daughter—would be persuaded to order three cupcakes per guest? Despite the smartest of calculations, who could have anticipated that these tiny colorful bites would cost the moon?

And easy? Convenient? Hah. Cupcake people spit on easy and convenient. They exist to bedevil you. Did you know you're supposed to have not one but at least two tasting appointments to pick fillings, frostings, flavors and flower garnishes? And that display options will rob you of sleep and haunt your dreams? What I discovered in the teeth of the Epic Battle of the Cupcakes was that there are as many flavors of cupcakes as there are ways to fight with your daughter—lavender infused, poppyseed vegan. Star anise meringue with goat cheese ganache. Twice-baked, half-baked, sushi cupcakes, you name it. They'll even want to create a "signature cupcake" for you. C'mon, *signature* cupcake? And even worse—you're supposed to taste them all.

I don' t know about you, but I never met a cupcake I didn't like. I don't need to schedule a damn meeting to determine that.

However.

What doesn't defeat you makes you stronger. I like to think I contributed to Elizabeth and Dave's strength as a couple by testing their will. If they can survive me in cupcake-hating-Momzilla mode, they can conquer the world.

Of all the things to get in a catfight about, the least likely will be the one that sneaks up on you and incites a flurry of fury. Honestly, cupcakes?

Never underestimate the power of a bride to overcomplicate things. After ~~an epic yelling match~~ a calm, reasoned discussion, it was agreed that there would be cake. Specifically, cupcakes. The perfect solution. They're cute, they're delicious, they're economical. They won't give the hotel staff a reason to charge some crazy catering fee. Guests will just pop them in their mouths and walk away with a smile.

Who knew a simple cupcake could turn into hours of debate?

Fortunately, the solution is simple. Trust your well-raised daughter to do the right thing. She will find the ideal purveyor of cupcakes. She will spend many long, obsessive hours deciding on which flavors to purvey. And on the wedding day, the little cakes will magically appear... and lo. They will be delicious.

CHEAT SHEET

DYING TO STUFF YOUR FACE WITH CAKE INSTEAD OF FINISHING THIS CHAPTER? HERE'S YOUR CHEAT SHEET:

1. While you still have the energy of a bride-to-be who hasn't reached her wedding saturation point, truck through some of the tedium (such as starting your guest list and compiling addresses).

2. Let's be honest: people probably won't remember what they ate at your wedding. I don't know about you, but I have trouble remembering what I ate for breakfast today. So choose food that speaks to you, and don't worry too much about what everyone else will think.

3. Keeping Rule #2 in mind, though, if your mother or some other VIP draws a line in the sand over a particular food selection, you might just wanna give in. Hell hath no fury like a mother starved.

11

MY YEAR OF BABE-IFICATION

Making sure you look your best
on your wedding day

ELIZABETH

Dear Readers, I do not naturally look as good as I did on my wedding day. Shocking, right? I used my wedding as a motivating force to build a healthy foundation for the rest of my life. Okay, that's what I told people. I really just wanted to look hot. Think about it: your wedding day will be the prettiest day of your life. It's all downhill from there. Just kidding—but it will be one of your most photographically documented days, so I put a high priority on reaching my full babe potential. For me, though, getting in shape for the wedding had an unanticipated benefit. It really did have an effect on my life.

Admit it: you want to look smokin' hot on your wedding day, too. Those pictures will be everywhere, you'll have an ex-boyfriend in the congregation, one of your bridesmaids weighs ninety-five pounds soaking wet and you have to dazzle everyone. And, hey, maybe you can spend your engagement developing a healthier lifestyle for yourself. Maybe, as your love grows for your future husband, you can also find a new love for yourself and for your bodacious bod. Just imagine it: your legs can climb mountains; your arms can give your fiancé a giant, crushing hug; your hands can carry bags from Macy's, Banana Republic AND Sephora without chipping your manicure.

I graduated from college with a lifelong athlete's breezy lack of concern about my figure. I had been on sports teams my entire life, so my normal routine included a daily three-hour swim workout fueled by a diet consisting of everything from bacon fries to cookie dough. This was working well for me...right up until I replaced my swim coach with a boss, my teammates with a cadre of coworkers and my team captain with a 6-foot-4, 165-pound Adonis of a fiancé.

Here's something nobody tells you about moving in with your man: he eats. He eats more than a gestating elephant.

So when you're preparing dinner together during those first bliss-ful months of cohabitation, you end up making two man-sized por-tions—and you split yours down the middle. At first, you eat half your serving and save the rest for lunch. One day, you'll be feeling extra hungry and you'll eat three-quarters of it. The next day, you'll do the same thing. Before you know it, you're on the slippery slope to eating as much as your man does, despite the fact that you're half his size and his metabolism runs circles around your own. One day, you step on the scale and realize that you're carrying around the weight equivalent of a small pony and you can't button your favorite jeans.

At least that's what happened to me. And if it doesn't happen to you, I don't want to hear about it because I'll have to shoot myself.

Still, there's a right way and a wrong way to get rid of your welcome-to-adulthood saddlebags. I'll tell you what I did, but the most important lesson you can learn from me is to learn what your rockin' bod needs from you. What worked for me might not work for you. The best you can do is sit quietly with yourself from time to time and take a minute or two to really listen to yourself.

It will be awkward at first—I mean, come on, who really buys that whole "my body is my temple" crap in the first place?—but find a way to be conscious of yourself. Once I started doing this, I noticed that I always felt uncomfortable and slightly comatose after every meal. I had started popping Tums like they were candy. Eventually, I figured out that it was because I shoveled food into my face like a madwoman who was afraid the imaginary voices in her head were going to steal her sustenance. So every time I sat down to dinner, I made a point of eating more slowly and pausing to savor my food. The next thing I knew, it had been a whole month and I couldn't remember the last time I'd felt the chalky, sugary texture of a Tums in my mouth.

I also noticed I was feeling lethargic and sleepy. I called my future mother-in-law, who is conveniently a doctor (seriously, try to marry into a family with a doctor—it is awesome), and she said it sounded like I wasn't getting enough exercise. My first reaction was to protest. If I wasn't getting enough activity, then what did she call my nightly cardio routine that consisted of striding from the couch to the refrigerator and back, carrying homemade hand weights fashioned from leftover containers of Thai food?

I think she must have talked to Dave about my concerns because I noticed that he slyly started asking me to go on runs with him. Then, for our anniversary, he gave me an endearingly girly shirt (isn't it funny how guys assume that if it's pink, we'll like it?), emblazoned with a photograph of us and the words "Team Awesome" across the chest. "I think we should run a half marathon together," he said, "and I made myself a matching shirt so we would have a team uniform."

Okay, all together now: AWWWWWWWWWWWWWWWWWW.

I've since talked to Dave about this and he insists that he was not using the half marathon as an excuse to get his fiancée to shed a little bit of her extra padding. I tend to believe him, since he wouldn't even notice if I dyed my hair black and pierced my eyebrows. He comes from an intimidatingly athletic family: his mother and two brothers are all marathon runners. He was just excited to get me to share another interest with him.

Well, people, we sat down and devised a training program for me. Over the course of three months, I slowly increased my long-distance runs until I could run ten miles without stopping.

I ran the Rock 'n' Roll half marathon in Seattle exactly one month before my wedding. Oh, and what a run it was. Twenty-five thousand people, a boatload of local bands and enough energy drinks to float a yacht. I even managed to rope Molly, my best friend and bridesmaid;

Dave's mom; and his brother into running the race as well. (Spoiler alert: I finished last among us, but that's to be expected of someone from the Wiggs clan. We're large and slow-moving, like glaciers.)

The night before the race, I found myself in a tizzy-fit of nerves. I'd been training for this race for months, calling my mother to whine about my aching legs and reminding myself that this was all worth it if it meant I looked gorgeous in my wedding dress. When I realized that in less than twenty-four hours I'd be completing a milestone that had once seemed as distant as my wedding, I had a little breakdown.

Dave found me crouched on the kitchen floor, eating brown sugar straight from the container with a spoon and crying.

This was new. He tried to pry the spoon from my sticky hands, but I jerked away from him and told him that I wasn't going to run the race tomorrow. He didn't even bother trying to convince me otherwise—he knew it was time to call in the big guns. He called my mom. I was not privy to the conversation, but according to him, she had one piece of advice: "Feed her, put her to bed and rub her back until she's asleep. It worked when she was two, and it'll work when she's twenty-five." Dave dropped everything and took me out for an ENORMOUS pasta dinner. He shoveled gnocchi and garlic bread into my face until I whimpered in protest, then whisked me home and tucked me into bed, staring at me anxiously with the eyes of a desperate man. He turned me on my side and commenced pawing at my back, unable to be gentle amid the swirling maelstrom of my stress.

But, oh boy, did it work.

Within five minutes, I was blissfully asleep, and when the alarm went off the next morning at the crack of dawn, I bounded out of bed, ready to take on the world.

The reality of the race hit me again as I took off my jacket and looked down at the T-shirt Dave had made, but this time the butterflies in my stomach came from knowing that I was about to run the half marathon I'd been training for, and that I was exactly one month from my wedding.

The race began and I was feeling pretty great. Awesome music was blasting over the loudspeakers and I felt light and loose on my feet. We got to the first band, and lemme tell you: live music during a race is inCRED. Every time I heard the strains of a rock song rolling back up the course toward me, I got a little bounce in my step and sped up so I could get to the band and hear what they were playing.

However. The route turned east and suddenly we were headed straight into the sun. This was approximately mile 3 (of thirteen), or right around the time I felt a painful tightness start to creep into my left knee. While the course wasn't very hilly overall, the first little bit of elevation turned the tightness into a gradually intensifying pain. At the next water station, I took a walking break and tried to give my leg a wee rest. "Holy crap," I thought, "I still have ten more miles of this misery and my knee is already giving me trubs. What am I going to dooooooooo?" (Yes, I did draw that syllable out into a howl in my head.)

Unfortunately, the five-second walking break didn't really do much for me (big surprise). I slowly came to understand that my knee was just going to get worse and worse. By mile 6, I felt like someone had shoved a knife up under my kneecap and was twisting it with glee.

And here's the moment I knew, beyond a shadow of a doubt, that in a month I would marry the best man on the face of the earth: sweet Dave stayed running alongside me this whole time, telling me how cute I looked and how excited he was for me. He never once breathed a word of complaint as I whined and cursed and lashed out at him. He didn't say a thing about the fact that he normally ran twice as fast as we were going. The next thing I knew, Dave reached out to put his arm around me and I burst into honking, messy tears.

I was so full of love at that moment—love for the man next to me, for the family and friends running the race with me, for my parents at home, tracking my progress on the race website. But I was also a little wistful. I realized, hobbling my way past the mile 8 marker, that part of my life—the part where I was the darling of my family, where my mother still thought of me as a little girl and was ready to swoop in at a moment's notice to help me clean up my messes—was about to come to a close. In one short month, I would enter the mystical world of married women. My mom and I would, for the first time in my life, share the same title. We would be Wives.

Normally the idea wouldn't be that emotional, but eight miles into a half marathon, with a knee screaming in pain, I had to slump down on the side of the road and have a little sob-fest.

As soon as he saw what was happening, Dave came straight back to my side and whispered, "This is going to be the hardest mile of the whole race, but as soon as we hit mile 9 you'll feel fine." I don't think he meant that to sound like a metaphor for our wedding, but it totally was. We were one month out—all the big pieces were in place, but we hadn't filled in the little last-minute gaps yet. The wedding seemed close enough to touch, yet everyone around me acted like four weeks was an eternity. The only other person who was feeling the pressure in the same way as me was my mom.

And oh, did I want my mommy at that moment.

But I was happy to settle for a caring, worried groom instead.

Dave ushered me to the medical station about five minutes later and gave me two Advils. I steeled myself against the pain in my knee and pushed ahead to what I knew would be the steepest hill of the entire race. Having gotten my head wrapped around the midrace wedding panic attack, I suddenly felt a renewed sense of excitement and optimism. As I ran the hill, I picked up speed.

And apparently I'm friggin' good at running uphill. I was passing people left and right, even with my knee pain, and by the time I got to the top I had left a whole army of suckers in my wake. At the hill's crest, we entered a tunnel—which apparently was full of Prozac-flavored air, because I suddenly felt GREAT and started skipping and cheering.

The next thing I knew, I had blown by the mile 10 marker and I was zooming past person after person. Dave laughed to see the change that had come over me (and I thought—but didn't say—that he should start getting used to my crazy mood swings). By the time we emerged from the tunnel, I was pretty much on drugs. That's how great I felt. The pain in my knee was still excruciating, but I didn't care.

Suddenly, I could see the finish line.

Talk about an adrenaline rush. As we rounded the bend, I could see the balloon arches marking the end of the race and I knew that, despite the knee, I would be able to push through the pain and run hard for the rest of the race.

I began to sprint as I ran down the ramp into downtown Seattle and could hear cheers reverberating across the entire city from the stadium where the finish line waited. I wanted to scream with exuberance, but I didn't because that would have been embarrassing and I like to pretend to have decorum sometimes.

Over the weeks leading up to the race, Dave and I had been finishing every practice run holding hands—to make sure that we looked good when we got to the end of the race. Well, folks, I screwed it up. About two hundred yards away from the finish line, Dave reached out and grabbed my hand and I suddenly burst into tears (again). In that moment, I thought I would explode from the love I felt for him. I was so proud of myself for finishing, and so thankful that My One did it with me. I fought to keep my sobs in check because I wanted to look pretty for the professional photo of us—but no luck. The result ended up being a picture of me half crying, half smiling, and was pretty high on the ugly scale. But in the photograph, you can also see the incredible feeling I had, knowing that my months of training and hard work had paid off.

A month later, I had the same ugly-yet-touching expression on my face as I walked down the aisle toward my groom.

I'm nothing if not consistent, I suppose.

So if you're a runner, you're probably wondering what my time was. I'll admit, I felt a little sheepish about how slow I was—but I had to keep reminding myself that I was new to the sport and hadn't really figured out a way to keep my body from breaking down on long runs. My overall time was a 2:15:13. Dave, whose best time in the half is a 1:13, made sure to point out that the race was a record for him, too— his Personal Worst. Har har, jerk. I guess he thought he could tease me after the crying and hysterics were over.

As we were leaving the stadium, I saw a guy wearing a shirt that said "Toenails are for sissies." With that in mind, I cannot write about my first half-marathon experience without including an ode to my right middle toenail, which lost its battle to remain a part of my foot after the race.

Middle toenail, I hardly knew ye. You managed to make it through months of training, but alas, the actual race was simply too much for your little body to bear. The entire tip of my toe became a blister full of blood and pus, and I knew that when it broke, you would ride off into the sunset, along with my ability to wear open-toed shoes. I mourned your loss, thanked my mother for her excellent taste in close-toed wedding shoes, and painted toe-nail polish on my skin on the day of my marriage so I didn't look like a weird, four-toenailed freak.

So there you have it. What started out as an attempt to get skinny for my wedding ended with an emotional race that reminded me how to find joy and energy in the whirlwind of the last month before my wedding. It was great. I laughed, I cried, I cried some more, I licked dried sweat off my upper lip and I lost my toenail. And I gained an appreciation for running, which is a skill that will keep me healthy for many years to come.

Okay, that last part is a lie. I still sort of hate running. But I can do it—and when my man is with me, it's not so bad. Most of the time.

Oh, and I won't complain about the twenty-five pounds I lost (and kept off), either.

CONFESSIONS OF A ZITTY BRIDE

Dear Readers, there's more to the beautification process than simply getting your bod in shape. My friends, let's not forget that beauty is skin-deep—meaning that you need the stuff on the outside to look great, too. (Oh, did I misinterpret the whole "skin-deep" thing? No? Didn't think so.)

Ever since I was little, I've had bad skin. I don't know what it is—apparently I did something awful in a past life, because I've been punished with acne-prone skin from a ridiculously young age. I've also developed the nasty-yet-totally satisfying habit of spending inordinate amounts of time exactly one inch from the mirror in the bathroom, squeezing the hell out of my pores. Don't act like you don't know what I'm talking about. The average person's nose is, from an inch away, rife with pores that are just begging to be poked and prodded for hours on end. We've all done it. And since we've all done it, we also know it usually makes the skin look worse than it would if we just left it the hell alone.

Still, I am proud to say that on my wedding day, I had smooth, clear skin. And that's a pretty big statement from me, queen of Accutane, a dermatologist's dream, who always has some sort of breakout or rash or allergic reaction to her own sweat. One of my biggest concerns as the wedding got closer was that I would walk down the aisle with a bumpy face. My makeup artist could conceal any redness, but what about the shadow from a Vesuvius-sized zit?

A month before the wedding, I called up the Medi-Spa at Virginia Mason Hospital in Seattle and made an appointment. I figured it would be better than a regular spa because it had "Medi" in the title. Also it was located in the hospital, so if I had some sort of extreme reaction to the coconut oil–infused acid mask they could rush me down the hall to the emergency room screaming, "BRIDE WITH BAD SKIN COMING THROUGH! WE NEED THE BEST DOCTOR IN THE HOSPITAL, STAT!"

As it turns out, they do not offer that service.

Luckily, though, I got set up with Diane—an angel who leaves strains of harp music in her wake—and she knew exactly what to do for me.

I'm not going to pretend to know the names of all the different lotions she put on my face, but by golly did they work. I went in to see her three times in about two weeks and after each appointment, my skin got a little better.

However.

Two weeks before the wedding, I went in for my last appointment. I plopped myself on the heated bed and turned my face toward the doughnut-shaped light-slash-magnifying glass.

Diane bent over my face and wiped my skin with some nice-smelling sponge thingy.

"This is not good," she said.

At first I was like, "What gives?" because I actually thought my skin was doing pretty well, considering. I mean, yeah, I was still a bit broken out but at least it wasn't red alert status, the way it had been two weeks ago.

But here's the thing about Diane: she's a perfectionist. And people, perfectionists are the best members to have on your team when you're a bride.

Diane wasn't going to settle for anything less than turning my face into a Neutrogena advertisement. She got up from her stool and strode out of the room, telling me that she would be back in a minute.

Turns out she went to the hospital's best dermatologist and told her about my plight. Apparently, the doctor took pity on me, a broken-out bride-to-be, and agreed to see me during her lunch break.

Since we had an hour to kill, Diane decided to pull out the big guns on my face. She gave me the facial to end all facials, a forty-five-minute experience that was so potent, so effective, so intense that I'm pretty sure I blacked out for part of it. No fewer than three masks were applied to my eruptive skin, along with countless different tonics and lotions that seeped into my pores and made me smell like a tropical fruit smoothie for the next week. Diane scrubbed, squeezed and mas-saged my face until my skin was forced to submit to her ways.

About ten minutes before the facial was over, Diane turned away from me. I had those cold little eye patch doodads on my lids, so I couldn't open my eyes to see what she was doing, but after a few seconds I could hear a crackling noise not unlike the sound bugs make when they hit the electric porch light and are zapped to death.

Diane draped my face in a thin gauze and told me to relax.

Although my eyes were closed, I could see bright blue flashes of light above my face, as though a blue strobe light had been turned on in the room. The next thing I knew, the zaps I had been hearing were landing on my face, stinging slightly and making frighteningly loud noises. I could smell the gauze on my skin burning slightly.

I won't lie: I got sort of freaked out.

Diane was using some high-frequency current wand to penetrate my skin's surface and kill all the bacteria lurking down there, waiting to ruin my wedding day. I was skeptical at first, but I looked in the mirror immediately afterward, and lo, my breakout had disappeared. It was a miracle! I was so happy that I told Diane I didn't think I needed to see the dermatologist, but she said I should still keep the appointment because I needed to continue to keep my face in check, even after the wedding.

Before I went into the dermatologist's office, though, Diane had a Serious Talk with me.

"You're a popper, aren't you?" she said gently.

I knew exactly what she meant, but I still feigned ignorance, hoping that unlike she had done on my face, she wouldn't be able to dig below the surface of my denial and extract the ugly truth. "I...don't know what you could possibly mean," I muttered in a strangled voice.

"Honey, I've seen your type before. You have fine, normal skin but you look at your pores in a magnifying mirror and squeeze them until they have no choice but to become blemishes."

I hung my head in shame.

"It's okay. I'm a popper, too. Why d'you think I'm in this profession?"

She had caught me zit-handed.

Crap.

Diane told me—and I'm relaying this to you, Dear Readers, because I absolutely don't believe you when you tell me that you haven't turned your nose into a porcupine of extractions before—that I needed to lay off the squeezing. Permanently.

After explaining that I was causing the majority of my skin problems, Diane ushered me into the dermatologist's office where I was prescribed a topical medication known for being gentle on the skin.

By the time my wedding rolled around, my face was as flawless as it had ever been. It was incredible. I never thought I would be able to put makeup on without devoting at least ten minutes to covering up red spots.

So, yeah, I'm embarrassed to reveal my love of squeezing pores, but I do so in the hopes that you might not have to go to a Medi-Spa a month before your wedding. (Although—aside from the scary-yet-awesome high-frequency light—it was pretty relaxing to get pampered a couple of times before the Big Day. I just wish I wasn't stressed the whole time about the efficacy of what I was putting myself through.)

The upshot is that now I know how to treat my skin, and I no longer torture it. Sure, that's about the most superficial thing a gal could possibly worry about, but having clear skin gives me confidence like you wouldn't believe. On my wedding day, my face was the last thing on my mind, and since then I've really turned over a new leaf, pore-wise. I'm like a new woman. I wouldn't be surprised if I get offered the presidency because my skin is so nice. I'm just saying.

But my skin was just the tip of the beautification iceberg. On the Wednesday before the wedding (aka the day before the day before the day before, but who would be silly enough to say something like that? Er...me), I set about putting the finishing touches on the tail end of a loooong process I like to call Operation Hot Bride.

First things first: I had to get ready for bathing suit weather on the h-moon. I had lost about twenty-five pounds and found the magic solution to getting clear skin, so next I needed to remove any, um, unsightly furriness from, you know, my armpits and other such areas. Ahem. Since I get a rash whenever someone looks at me funny, shaving and waxing weren't really options—so I decided to try this process called sugaring.

Dear Readers, if you have not tried sugaring, you have not lived. My pits—they were hairless. My skin—it was smooth as a baby's butt. My life—it was changed. Here's the deal: sugaring is the process of hair removal using a paste made from sugar and lemon juice. It's applied at room temperature—rather than at the scaldingly hot temperature of melted wax—and since it's all natural, the paste only sticks to dead skin cells and hair. You know that feeling during waxing when she yanks off a particularly stubborn strip and you could SWEAR that your skin came with it? Doesn't happen during sugaring. There are lots of other technical details I could get into for you, but honestly, all you need to know is that I walked out of my session with Erica at Jill Bucy Skincare in Seattle and I couldn't tell that I'd had anything done. I wasn't sore or itchy, as I always am after waxing and shaving. And I had zero ingrown hairs. Zero! Do you understand me?! I'm usually a WALKING ingrown hair!

Sugaring wasn't the only new thing I tried before the wedding. Ohhhhh no. See, Erica, the gal who did my sugaring, had these amazing eyelashes. I was obsessed with them as soon as I saw her. And I figured that since she was, you know, ripping hair out of my body, she wouldn't mind if I asked her what the deal was. Her eyelashes were long as a harbor seal's but they weren't fake—I couldn't see a strip or a drop of glue anywhere.

It turns out that she had eyelash extensions. Long story short, that afternoon I found myself on my back in a salon for three-and-a-half hours getting synthetic eyelashes individually applied to my natural ones. One hundred forty per eye, to be exact. I am not exaggerating when I say that my eyelashes had their own silhouette. I didn't even need sunglasses because of the shadow they cast on my eyes.

The best part about eyelash extensions? They fall out with your natural eyelashes. That means I got to look gorge for four to six weeks.

Yep, sugaring and eyelash extensions—who knew? Now, I'll tell you right off the bat: neither procedure is cheap. Sugaring costs about the same as waxing at a spa (as opposed to waxing at a nail salon) and eyelash extensions start at around $150 or $200 and go up from there, depending on how much drama you're looking for. But if you divide the cost out by the number of days that you're gorge, and add to it the hours of makeup time you save, it's not that bad, right?! RIGHT?! TELL ME IT'S OKAY TO SPEND HUNDREDS OF DOLLARS ON EYELASHES. It's not, but hey, it was my wedding.

CHEAT SHEET

AFTER COUNTLESS HOURS OF MEDITATION ON MY OWN WEDDING LOOK, I CAN NOW SUM UP MY THOUGHTS AS FOLLOWS:

1. Don't starve yourself or choose a hair/makeup style that will make you look like a different person on your wedding day. You want to be the most beautiful version of yourself—you're not getting in shape for your wedding; you're getting in shape for your life.

2. Looking back, even though my motivation was pure vanity, I did get myself back to my natural weight, and I finally felt comfortable in my own skin.

3. Sometimes you just need a panic-inducing situation to give you the kick in the pants you need to stop squeezing your nose pores in the mirror and get your booty to the gym.

12

A VERY
IMPORTANT DATE

Your wedding time line, and why you'll
probably throw that time line out the
window on the Big Day

ELIZABETH

See, here's the thing about weddings that nobody ever really seems to mention: all those guests are there for you. I guess nobody mentions it because saying it out loud sounds so obvious, but for me, there were about five separate times during the wedding weekend where I looked around at all the people who had made the trek to Seattle and said to myself, "They're all here because of Dave and me... whoa." It wasn't necessarily a good or a bad feeling...just...weird. The realization really didn't hit me, though, until the night before the wedding, when Dave's family hosted a happy hour at Kells, our favorite pub in Seattle.

I'd also like to point out that I had zero to do with the planning of that whole shindig. I left the menu up to Dave, and I'll be damned if he didn't do a fantastic job. Everyone was happy. But first let's rewind to the beginning of that day.

Our wedding planners had a morning of pampering planned for me and a couple of my bridesmaids, so I spent a luxurious few hours getting my nails and hair done. I got my finger and toenails painted in a color called "Mimosas for the Mr. and Mrs." by OPI. (Aubrey, my bridesmaid, invitation designer and guru of taste and style, supplied it.)

The color is a beautiful milky pink that I NEVER would have picked off the shelf. All I knew was that I wanted my nails to look like the inside of a seashell—and they totally did. Yvonne, our photographer, said

THE BIG DAY

Our wedding was carefully orchestrated down to the minute, starting two days before. Our wedding planners created the mother of
all time lines for us, but gave it to us with a cautionary word: "This
will get you off on the right foot," Jody said, "but we're going to
get off track. So think of this like a set of movable pieces—there
might come a time when we have to reorder or completely toss
out some stuff." I think she was worried that I would memorize the
whole thing and then spend the entire wedding weekend staring
at a clock, issuing angry commands when our events started to
run late. I don't blame her—I'm pretty neurotic. But as the wedding drew closer, a Zen-like calm descended over me and I peace-
fully let Jody and her team guide me. It was blissful. Probably not
for them—we definitely ran into a couple of bumps in the road—
but I managed to remain serene the whole time.

In general, here was the outline of our timeline:

7:30 a.m. — bride wakes up, eats breakfast and gets started with
hair and makeup

10:30 a.m. — groom and groomsmen get together to begin the
tuxedoing process

Noon — bride, bridesmaids and bride's parents have a photo
shoot—then back to the hotel for lunch and little bit
of down-time

1:00 p.m. — groom, groomsmen and groom's parents have a
photo shoot

2:30 p.m. — bride and groom arrive separately at the venue and
are hidden from one another

3:00 p.m. — guests start arriving

3:30 p.m. — ceremony starts

4:45 p.m. — bride and groom leave for portraits, guests depart
for reception venue and have a cocktail hour until
the happy couple returns

6:00 p.m. — bride and groom make grand entrance to a rockin'
song and much fanfare

7:00 p.m. — party tiiiiiiiiiiiiiime!

Midnight — bride and groom depart, bow-chicka-bow-bow, and
guests continue the party in the suite of a very generous groomsman

afterward that she was so glad I had a pretty manicure so she could take loads of ring photos. Also, while I'm at it, I gotta make a pitch for getting a professional mani-pedi. My manicure lasted without a scratch for a full two-and-a-half weeks after the wedding until I finally needed to cut my nails because I was starting to look like that lady in the Guinness Book of World Records who has nails so long they curl.

After getting my fingers and toes done, including the toenail-less tootsie, I headed back to our hotel to meet the most incredible, amazing, magnificent hairstylist of all time. Jacquelynn, whom I introduced to you in Chapter 7, was the hair prodigy behind my night-before and day-of wedding hair. Using a flat iron and the eye of a master artiste, she styled my locks in smooth, loopy curls. In hindsight, I would recommend that all brides ask their hair peeps what they should do to and with their hair the night before the wedding—Jacquelynn told me exactly which products to put in and even if she hadn't styled my hair the night before, my tresses would have been properly prepped for the updo the following day.

The result? My hair the night before and the day of the wedding looked like a shampoo commercial.

Suddenly, as I slipped into my night-before outfit—a cream-colored, eyelet lace sundress and open-toed ivory pumps—I could see why women get postwedding depression. There was just no way I would ever look like that again...unless I moved back to Seattle and forced Jacquelynn and her husband to live with me and Dave, made a gazillion bucks to buy only tailored Anthropologie dresses and found a way to stay permanently in shape.

We arrived at Kells early to run through the wedding rehearsal. Talk about a head game. I felt like I was on drugs the whole time. Wedding drugs. I think the technical name is "less than twenty-four hours until I get married" drugs. As my dad and I practiced walking down the aisle and executing the father-to-groom bridal handoff, my chest constricted with the reality of what was about to happen. I was getting married tomorrow.

I looked around me. To either side of our makeshift altar fashioned from a tall bar table, I could see our bridesmaids and groomsmen—friends who had been handpicked to stand here with us during this moment. This was the first time I'd seen them in the same room together, and the weight of their love and support hit me in the face like a cream pie. Behind me, Dave's and my parents sat together looking eager, nervous and a little queasy. My mom in particular.

We began to walk through the ceremony, and when we got to the vows, our officiant asked us to just say the first line to each other. "I, Elizabeth Anne Wiggs, come here today to join my life to yours as your wife," he prompted me.

I opened my mouth.

I couldn't speak.

My voice was being choked off by a large lump that had grown in my throat as we paced out our wedding ceremony.

I glanced over my shoulder and met my mom's eyes. I could tell from her expression that she was feeling the exact same lump.

I gulped a shaky breath and managed to spit out my line without letting the tears in my eyes fall down my cheeks, and our practice ceremony continued. The rest of the rehearsal passed in a blur—part of me floated above the whole thing, looking down and thinking, "Is this seriously happening?" The part of me that was present in the moment felt every touch, every breath, with such intensity that I knew I would never forget these minutes. The butterflies in my stomach fluttered to life, then quieted, then fluttered again with no real rhyme or reason.

I was getting married tomorrow.

Tomorrow, I would be Dave's wife.

Suddenly, people I hadn't seen in years started pouring through the doors of the dimly lit pub for the happy hour Dave had planned and, just like that, our wedding weekend began. I spent the rest of the evening saying hi to old friends and having occasional panic attacks in the bathroom. It was awesome. Every once in a while, one of my bridesmaids would find me and make sure I was holding up okay. Molly was especially alert to this, having been through it less than a year before. She had no problem muscling her way into a conversation I was having with Dave's aunts, squaring out like a linebacker and saying gruffly, "Eat this" as she stuffed a forkful of penne pasta into my mouth.

Most of the photos taken of me that night reveal an I'm-keeping-it-together-but-I-may-have-just-messed-myself smile.

But then I would look over and see Dave and his brothers, or my best friend from childhood, or my mom with her brother and sister, and I would feel calm and ready to board the wedding train. Dave and I stepped outside for some air and we found ourselves in a sunbeam. I took it as a sign from the benevolent wedding gods. This was going to be fun. I was overwhelmed, excited, nervous and pretty damn gorgeous, if I do say so myself.

As the happy hour began to wind down, Dave and I left and went to Seattle's Olympic Sculpture Park for our last moments alone as an unmarried couple. Friends and family asked where we were going as we walked away, but we just smiled and kept silent. Dave would be back to join the party soon, we told them, and I'd see everyone tomorrow.

I passed my mom on the way out. She pulled me in for a crushing hug, then held me at arm's length and said, "Baby, I'm so proud of you."

"I'll see you in the morning, Mommy," I said. I could feel the lump threatening to clog my throat again, but I swallowed it down and smiled at her.

Both of us had been so distracted by all the friends and family arriving that we'd barely had a moment to talk to each other. But we didn't need to. I knew she was experiencing my feelings as her own. When I was a baby, she would magically wake seconds before I did each morning, hurrying into my room to be with me as my eyes opened because she felt my separation anxiety as keenly as if she were the one who was deathly afraid of being left alone. We were connected without having to talk about it, because I was as much a part of her as her right arm. She reached down, grabbed my hand and gave it two quick squeezes—a gesture she'd been doing since I was little to give me courage. I waved to her and turned to my almost-husband.

Dave and I got to the park and found a table under an awning. The place was deserted except for a few joggers and their dogs. As we watched the sun go down over Puget Sound, we read each other the personal vows we'd written in private that were too deep to share in front of an audience during our wedding ceremony. Dave read his vows with a shaky voice while tears of happiness and emotion poured down my face, and by the time I read what I had written we were both crying openly, bowled over by the end of our lives as single individuals and the beginning of our marriage. Here are the vows we wrote to each other, in their entirety:

My dearest Dave,

Tonight, the night before we become husband and wife...

KIDDING. (Somewhere out there my husband just totally FREAKED out.) Nobody will ever know what we said to one another. It's important for every couple to have secret promises. You never know when you might have to cling to those promises as your only life raft in a sea of pain and struggle together. For me, making them only to Dave—without anyone else watching—made them much more profound and binding. I liked doing this the night before the wedding, which was also the last time we would see or speak to each other until we met before our officiant the next day, but it's never too late to tell your One exactly why you're going to stick by him or her forever and ever.

It was also a GREAT way to get some of the tears out of our systems, even though the next day I sobbed my way to the altar like a little baby. Yeesh.

After I wiped the tears from my face, Dave walked me to the street and put me in a car. We kissed—our last kiss before we were married—and he smiled at me. "See you tomorrow," he said.

It was a pretty intense "See you tomorrow." My stomach did a cartwheel-back-handspring-round-off and stuck the landing.

I told the cab to take me to the hotel, and Dave turned and walked back to the pub, where our party-happy friends were getting ready to paint the town. I don't know much about what happened while I wasn't there, but I've heard rumors of bathtubs full of booze, a friend doing the worm in the middle of a dance floor and a stolen unicycle. I won't lie— I'm pretty proud of my friends. They know how to do things right.

At that moment, though, I wasn't thinking about the drunken antics being performed in my honor. I was getting married tomorrow. *I was getting married tomorrow.* CRIPES, I WAS GETTING MARRIED TOMORROW!

The taxi dropped me off at the hotel—I gave the driver a 300 percent tip—and I skittered up to my room. Inside, I found my three best friends, Molly, Lindsey and Aubrey. We spent the rest of the night eating pizza and executing the age-old girly slumber party activity of giggling and talking about sex. And my girls watched over me like mother hens, doing their best to stand in for my mom, who was wrangling extended family members at her own house. Aubrey, the wedding expert among us, told me to chug water to stay hydrated and commanded me to sleep on my back so I didn't get creases on my face from the pillowcase. Lindsey, the most organized, laid out my robe, shoes and jewelry for the next day. Molly, the nurturer of our group, put together a bag of snacks for tomorrow and made sure the hotel knew what I wanted for breakfast in the morning.

It was perfect.

I fell asleep with no trouble, my mind calm with an undercurrent of excitement and nerves.

In the morning, the sun fell across my lids and woke me at 6:30. I rolled over and saw that Molly, lying next to me, was also awake.

"It's your wedding day," she whispered.

My wedding day. It was my wedding day.

Excitedly, I put on my robe and slippers and took the Luna Bar Molly held out for me. Aubrey told me to put on lip balm to make my lips supple for the makeup artist, and we trooped out of the room to the elevator for a ride up to the hotel's stunning penthouse suite, where we would be getting ready.

I felt calm and happy.

The elevator doors opened and inside was a girl about our age, wearing a lime-green, satin gown and matching shoes. She smiled at us, her freshly made-up face glowing warmly. *She can tell it's my wedding day*, I thought. *I must be emitting bride signals!*

I reached out to press the elevator's "PH" button to take us to the top floor, where the sixteen-hundred-square-foot bridal suite waited, but stopped because the button was already illuminated. It was like the universe could read my mind!

We rode to the top floor, and when the doors opened, the girl in the lime-green dress stepped out with us. *She must be staying on this floor, too*, I thought.

Molly, Lindsey, Aubrey and I started walking down the hallway toward the suite. We were a little early and knew that nobody else— the makeup artist, the hairstylist, my mom, the other bridesmaids— would be there yet, but we were going to call room service and have our breakfast delivered.

As we rounded the corner, I could see the elegant double doors to the suite. I paused, realizing we didn't have a key to the room yet. As I turned to ask one of my girls to run down and grab a key from the front desk, I spotted the girl in the lime-green dress.

Her hair was piled on top of her head in an elaborate updo and I got a lovely view from the back as she stepped by us, murmuring, "Excuse me" and flashing one last smile.

Wait—why was she passing us? The only room in this hallway was the bridal suite.

She reached into a clutch made from the same lime-green satin as her dress and shoes and pulled out a key card.

I felt the air whoosh out of my lungs as she popped the key into the slot on the door of the bridal suite—*my bridal suite*—and pushed the handle.

As the doors swung open, I looked inside. Eight girls wearing identical lime-green dresses twittered around another young woman in a robe just like mine, sipping a mimosa and having her hair done.

My mind was blank with confusion. I didn't understand what was happening until Aubrey spoke. "It's another bride," she said flatly.

Another bride?

Another bride?!

There I was, in the buff under my robe, being punched in the face with the news that my precious princess suite had been invaded by an enemy bride and her disgustingly well-coordinated bridesmaid minions.

Now, many brides would probably have reacted with tears of sadness, fists of rage or squeals of cosmic pain. I waited for my own reaction.

But it never came. Calmly, I turned to my friends and said, "Okay! Let's go talk to the front desk!"

Fifteen minutes later, we figured out that the rogue bridal party had called late last night and booked the room through a night receptionist who didn't know it was reserved for the following morning.

Thirty seconds after that, Jody and her wedding squad swarmed into the lobby of the hotel, ready to do battle. I don't know what she said to the people at the hotel, but the next thing I knew I was ensconced in a limo, being whisked away to a suite at the Four Seasons, where I would be getting ready instead.

Was it as roomy as the original bridal suite? No.

Did I give a rip? Definitely not.

I still got to be surrounded by my girls and my mom as I got buffed and fluffed.

I still got to sit quietly and slowly ease into the most important day of my life.

I still got to run an IV line of champagne into my bloodstream.

Sure, the whole episode with the doppelgänger bride put us

behind schedule by about an hour, and we took fewer bridal portraits with my bridesmaids. Ultimately, we ended up running out of time for family portraits, something I still regret. But our photographer managed to take incredible candid shots of all my loved ones enjoying the wedding. And I would take the genuine smiles and emotion in those photographs over plastered-on, posed portraits any day.

The hotel, of course, was profusely apologetic about the whole situation, but I was happy to forgive. It was an innocent mistake—and they more than made up for the issue by offering a ton of freebies the next time we stayed there.

The moral of the story? Something will go wrong. Accept it, move on and practice saying "So what?" when someone makes a mistake. Or sic your mom on the offender. I didn't have to pull out the mother-guns on the hotel, but don't think for a second that she wasn't ready to rip open someone's jugular with her French manicure on my command.

SUSAN

There was a moment when we were getting ready for the big entrance, putting the finishing touches on hair and makeup, poofing the dress, straightening the pearls, putting the veil in place, when a thoughtful expression softened Elizabeth's face. "This is my prettiest day," she said. "I'll never be prettier than I am today. It's all downhill from here."

And I thought, *Oh, honey.*

Far be it from me to tell the bride on her wedding day that she's wrong. She'll discover it on her own, anyway.

It's true that every happy bride is beautiful. But her prettiest day? Not even close.

Because here's the truth. When you find the love of your life, the puzzle piece that completes you, the one person who gives you that deep sense of joy, then every day is your prettiest day.

Each morning when you get up, he will look at you and something magical will happen. No matter what day it is, he will see true beauty. As time goes by, your beauty will only deepen and intensify in his eyes. This includes—but is not limited to—mornings when you're late and yelling at him and racing to catch the bus. Late nights when you've stayed up, arguing about nothing. When you're eight months' pregnant and bloated like a tick. When you're crying over a lost cat or fighting with your mother. And when you turn forty, and seventy-three, and when you win an award or crash the car or you're sick in bed or grieving a loss. To the love of your life, those are *all* your prettiest days.

Today is just the first of many such days, and I'm glad I got to witness it.

Maybe those really were your prettiest shoes, though. Man, those wedding shoes were something.

CHEAT SHEET

PREOCCUPIED WITH MAKING SURE YOUR OFFICIANT BEGINS THE CEREMONY PRECISELY TWENTY-SEVEN SECONDS AFTER 3:34 P.M.? HERE'S YOUR CHEAT SHEET:

1. Okay, yeah, something will probably go wrong on your wedding day. I had heard this before, but I tried to convince myself that my day was so well planned-out that everything would go off without a hitch. But I also learned that nothing—*nothing*—will keep you from ending up married to your partner in the end. Unless you leave him standing at the altar. Um...so don't do that. Put down the paper bag you're hyperventilating into and listen to me: No matter what happens, it will be your wedding day. You have my permission to write me a vicious email if your wedding day isn't the happiest day of your life to date (apparently there will be even more awesome days...I'm still waiting on that one).

2. It's great to have a wedding timeline, but don't get so attached to it that you'll break out in hives when things get a little behind schedule.

3. In the hours leading up to and during your wedding day, try to remain conscious of the moment. You won't recognize most life-changing events until after they're over—but your wedding day is a chance to reflect on the cosmic shift you're experiencing as it happens. Take advantage. Keep your eyes open, and cherish every second.

13

THE CEREMONY

Oh, yeah! You're actually going
to end up married! The moment
you'll become husband and wife

ELIZABETH

It's called a wedding because two people are getting married—you and your One. Try to keep this in mind when you're freaking out about the lining in your bridesmaids' shoes.

In the months leading up to the wedding, I started having flashbacks to stories my married friends had told me. While the details varied, an anecdote I'd heard over and over was the one about the first step down the aisle: "I had been WIGGING out all day," said one coworker. "But as soon as I saw my guy at the end of the aisle, I forgot all my worries and stayed calm for the whole ceremony."

The vast majority of the wives had a story about an unexpected change that had come over them as they began that long, slow walk toward their future husbands. I didn't give it much thought until my own wedding drew near, but suddenly I found myself obsessing over what profound shift I would experience as I turned the corner and saw Dave standing at the altar, waiting for me in front of all our guests. I envisioned my whole range of emotions and tried to guess where I would end on the spectrum. Would I be as calm and graceful as my friend, Molly, had been, smiling radiantly at various audience members to my left and right as I walked down the aisle? Would I gaze steadily and confidently at my future husband, as Dave's cousin had? Would I smile through a glistening veil of tears? Grin and laugh at the wonder of the moment? Silently mouth "I love you" at Dave? Pause and embrace my parents and grandparents? Hold myself like a regal queen, secure in her power and womanhood?

Notice that in all these ruminations, the bride is doing something meaningful and touching.

She's definitely not embarrassing herself or anything like that.

I never even considered the possibility that I would screw up the walk down the aisle.

Okay, so throughout the day leading up to the 3:00 p.m. wedding, I was chill as a cucumber. I calmly glided through the hotel room confusion, through unseasonably hot weather, through emotionally charged moments with my mom. Moments before I walked down the aisle, I sat in a back room with my dad making jokes and sipping champagne to calm the butterflies in my stomach. But I felt serene. Collected. Ready.

Jody, our wedding planner, poked her head in the door and said, "It's time."

I looked at my dad, grinned, took a deep breath and walked down the hall that led to the atrium where I would be getting married.

I tucked my hand into the warm crook of Daddy's arm as I approached the end of the aisle. Nobody could see me yet, but I could hear the strains of "Morning Has Broken" by Cat Stevens beginning to play. Jody quickly reached out and positioned my bouquet of white hydrangea, fluffed my train and smiled at me.

We turned the corner. I looked up and saw a room of nearly two hundred people, all looking at me. At the end of the aisle in front of me, beneath a gauzy white canopy, I saw Dave.

And I lost it.

Not just a little.

With a snort, I heaved out a giant sob.

Inside my head, the alarm bells went off. *Wait, you were calm just a second ago! Stop! Stop crying! You KNOW you have an ugly cry face! Don't ruin the photos!*

Impulsively, I jerked my hand—the one holding the bouquet—up to my face, a lame attempt to hide from two hundred pairs of eyes looking at me. I glanced at the DJ to my right. What did I think I was going to do? Make him stop the music and start the whole thing over again?

Crap, I thought. *I suck.*

I choked out a couple more sobs—the squeaky, high-pitched kind—and gulped in a huge breath of air. *Smile through the glittering veil of tears!* I desperately told myself. I tried to wrench the sides of my mouth upward, but my cheeks quivered and fought the effort, my tearful pout overpowering any attempt to look pretty. I bit the inside of my lips and attempted to force my face into submission, but no avail.

All this happened in the span of about three seconds.

My dad looked down at me with a worried expression as he felt my first step on the aisle waver.

Suddenly, I realized how silly my internal monologue was.

So I was going to sob down the aisle. So what? Sure, maybe I'd look like a medieval wench with a sizable dowry being forced into an arranged marriage, but whatever. It was my wedding. These would all turn into fond memories.

Four seconds.

I lowered my bouquet and looked up at Dave. I held his gaze as best I could through my streaming tears while I clutched my dad's arm and continued my walk down the aisle. Out of the corner of my eye, I saw my friend Ashley crying with me, and as I passed her I muttered, "I'm not gonna make it!"

I don't know what I meant. Not going to make it down the aisle? Not going to make it through the wedding without crying? Not going to make it out of this crazy world alive?

I don't know, but I heard Ashley laugh and I felt the butterflies in my stomach settle. I smiled at Dave as best I could, and before I knew it I was standing in front of him at the altar.

I turned to my dad and listened to him respond, "Her mother and I do," when our officiant asked who brought this woman to be given to this man.

I won't lie; my dad looked pretty miserable.

My dad's one of those guys who panics when his little girl cries. He never knows what to do with all the emotion, with the wrenching heartstrings, with the sprinkler system that has just started to squirt out of his daughter's face.

I caught his eye and pointed to the very top of my head, a gesture I've done since I was little—a silent demand for a kiss on the head. He leaned forward and planted one on me, reached out and shook Dave's hand, then helped me step up onto the dais.

This was it. The wedding had begun.

I dabbed at the tears under my eyes with my handkerchief, took Dave's hands and turned to our officiant to listen to his comments on the nature of marriage.

The rest of the ceremony was most definitely not a blur, though I know some brides say theirs was. I remember every second of the thirty-odd minutes that turned me into a wife. I remember the audience laughing as I wiped a bead of sweat from Dave's cheek (it was ninety-six degrees and he was in a tuxedo—can you blame the guy?). I remember glancing over Dave's shoulder and seeing his dad wink at me. I remember being the only one who noticed the single tear that fell down Dave's cheek as his cousins and uncle performed an acoustic arrangement of "In My Life" by the Beatles. I remember our best friends, Molly and Jesse, carefully leading us through a hand-holding ceremony that I had planned on having in my wedding since high school. I remember hugging Molly after she finished her reading and whispering "Oh, my God!" into her ear because I could barely contain myself. I remember the feeling of tears filling my eyes as I began to say my vows to Dave, forcing me to pause and collect myself so I could get through them without barfing emotion all over him. I remember Dave's great-uncle talking about breaking my hymen—yep, someone said *hymen* during my wedding ceremony—before Dave and I performed the Jewish glass-stomping ceremony. I remember seeing my dad shaking with laughter at the word *hymen*. I remember the overwhelming feeling of hearing *man and wife* as we turned toward the audience and walked out of the auditorium. And I remember looking at my mom and seeing her face wreathed in such joy that I knew—despite all the head-butting and strife—she was proud of me, proud of my husband and proud of the beautiful wedding we had created together.

It was awesome.

And remember the whole ugly, photo-ruining sobbing down the aisle crisis?

Weeks later, I got my wedding photographs and video back, and it turns out that my "ugly cry" wasn't so ugly after all. Sure, I looked emotional and had the teensiest bit of a double chin when I ducked my head shyly in an attempt to hide my tears. But mostly I look like a beautiful, emotional bride who had just been hit by the significance of the moment.

I had nothing to worry about.

And that's my advice to you, brides: if you're hit with some random emotion or feeling that you weren't expecting during your wedding ceremony, ride it out. Don't think about it or worry about what it will look like in your photographs. The love you're feeling will make you beautiful, no matter what.

Plus, if it's really that bad (and it won't be), there's always Photoshop.

SUSAN

THE BIG DAY HAS ARRIVED!

"Can I have a bagel? Wait, I'd rather have an English muffin, with freezer jam."

"Where's the dustpan?"

"What's your wireless password again? I need to check my email."

"Is Barkis allowed to eat that?"

"Is there a dry cleaner nearby?"

"The printer's jammed and I need to print the MapQuest directions."

"We're out of coffee."

"The dog just yarked on the carpet."

"You never told me I'd need cuff links."

"Can I borrow your hair dryer? And will you iron this shirt?"

"Someone's at the door."

Let's hope it's an ax murderer. Because, face it, as much as you adore your family and have been dreaming of a houseful o' love for this blessed event, you kind of want them dead right now. All of them, right down to the little old lady rooting around in the fridge for the jar of Marmite.

It's your daughter's damn wedding day. Doesn't anyone appreciate that?

Fortunately, I have a completely nonfelonious solution for dealing with a situation like this—and trust me, it will come up. Four words: *Run Away From Home.*

Yes, I mean it. Smile excitedly, check your watch or cell phone screen and say, "I have to go now. I've got a hair appointment."

"At 7:00 in the morning?" Skeptical frowns all around.

"The hairdresser insisted. She's giving me a special process." Lie with impunity. No one will quibble with a hairdresser's special process. Then say, "I'll see you at the ceremony!"

Breeze out of there, jump in the car and floor it.

A couple of assumptions. Prior to making your great escape, you have done everything on your mental and/or written checklist. You have your dress, shoes, jewelry and makeup already stashed in the car. (Note: You have my permission to forget your Spanx—you know, those punishing undergarments that suck everything in. No one will think less of you for it.)

Grab your purse (take the cell phone, but turn the ringer off for now) and drive. Where you go is up to you. Just make sure it's peaceful, quiet and unknown to people in need of English muffins or freezer jam. Stop at a latte stand and get yourself something tall, sweet and creamy. Make sure you have a fat, juicy novel to read.

I really did have a hair appointment the morning of the wedding. Not at 7:00 a.m., though. So what I did was, I got my double-tall-skinny-vanilla and took it to the waterfront park, which at that hour was deserted except for some really quiet people doing tai chi, and a Border Collie stalking some killdeer. I stood watching the sky turn from pink to gold, and I pictured my daughter at every phase of her life—every beautiful, naughty, glorious, frustrating, hilarious, triumphant, despairing and joyous moment of her life—and with every cell of spiritual energy I had, I wished her well. And had a little cry.

Okay, kind of a big cry.

Then I got over myself, went and sat on the front porch of the salon and did my nails. A French manicure with seashell pink. (Tip: Always try to patronize a beauty shop that has a front porch.)

Take some deep breaths. Don't touch anything until the nail polish sets hard. And for heaven's sake, quit fretting. Don't worry about abandoning your family, your houseguests, even your stubbornly clueless spouse. It's not your job to manage everything. That's what you do every other day of your life.

You need to take time on the day of the wedding that's just for you. You need to remember this is a spiritual, life-changing event, not to be taken lightly, so give it the time and space it deserves.

As for the above-mentioned spouse, you probably have one of your own. Maybe you've had him for decades and you're *still* not done raising him. That's because—news flash, hello—he's a *guy*. He is not going to turn into Richard Gere in *Shall We Dance?* overnight. Or ever, for that matter.

Just remind yourself of this—you'll be surprised at how well he comports himself, left to his own devices. Maybe the pleats of his cummerbund will be facing down. It's quite possible he's wearing zip-ties where the cuff links are supposed to be. And, um, you might catch a glimpse of athletic tube sock peeking out of his tux shoe. I'm just saying.

But again, remember, a joyous smile covers a multitude of flaws. This is the guy who helped you raise the princess bride. He's fabulous, when it comes down to it. My editor and friend, Margaret, had a great suggestion I wish I'd taken—after the postwedding dust settles, jump in the car with this guy and head out for your own little recovery-moon. That comes later. For now, though, just get him into some semblance of a tux and hope for the best.

Better yet, take advantage of all available family members. It would be a great idea to leave him in the care of your two most ir-resistible nieces. Honestly, have you ever known him to say no to his nieces?

Tell the nieces that the hairstylist is supposed to make him look like Dr. McDreamy on *Grey's Anatomy*. Tell them they must not allow him to smoosh down his hair with his lucky baseball cap. Tell them there must not be any visible duct tape anywhere on his person. Tell them his socks need to be black, even if it means getting out the Sharpie markers.

Style tip: The best wardrobe Nazi in the world is a twelve-year-old niece.

ELIZABETH

One intrinsic wedding detail that many couples seem to do the night before is the writing of the ceremony. Writing your ceremony should be a personal process involving you, your fiancé and your officiant. Oh, and if your mom is a romance writer, guess who else gets a say? Luckily for us, words (even the words of a published novelist) are cheap and asking for her input didn't lead to another showdown between the Wiggs women. Honestly, at that point, as long as I wasn't asking my mom for more money, she was happy.

The ceremony came together somewhat seamlessly—it's pretty awesome having a family of writers. And our officiant provided us with the most customizable of templates so that we could incorporate any extra elements that we wanted. Michael, the man who married us, was a friend of my dad's who was deeply intellectual and spiritual, a perfect fit since neither Dave nor I wanted our wedding to reflect a particular religion. Michael didn't even mind that I refused to have the phrase *till death do us part* uttered during our ceremony. Because, I don't know about you, but death will be nothing more than a speed-bump for Dave and me. Spiritual beliefs aside, if there is a heaven, I'm not about to show up there, see Dave and be, like, "Oh, uh, about that life we spent together...? Yeah. Uh, I don't know if you remember our, ahem, *agreement,* but I think I'm going to go on a casual date with this angel I met the other day..."

It might sound stupid to you, but Michael didn't bat an eyelash when I told him my reasoning for using the phrase *forever and ever* instead of *till death do us part.*

SUSAN

Moments before the ceremony, I considered drawing Elizabeth aside for one final mother-daughter chat before she headed out on her epic trek down the aisle. In the meltdown room, we would lovingly embrace and I would tell her...what? After all this time, and all the planning and advice and arguments and hilarity, what on earth was left to say? That I love her? (Duh.) That I'm proud of her and excited for all the future holds? (Again, duh.)

The truth is, by the time this moment arrives, there is nothing left to say. She knows it all. You know she knows. Flogging the issue one last time is only going to make you both cry and ruin your makeup. Now your job is to simply walk down the aisle, take your seat in the front row and get out your hankie.

But still, be prepared to have a pang. There will come a moment when everything stops, like the wind taking a breath in the middle of a storm, and it hits you right in the solar plexus—your daughter's life is heading off in a different direction, *away* from you.

There might be this searing thought: *no bloody way*. You want to grab the groom by his big, flapping ears and say, "Forget about it. I changed my mind. You can't have her. She's mine. I put twenty-five years of blood, sweat and tears into this child and you're not about to take her away."

I bet lots of moms feel this way. Of course you don't want to let go. She's your heart, your life, your soul, and there's no way you're sharing her.

These feelings are normal. And, trust me, they will pass, blown away by the winds of change. I'm not being a Pollyanna when I tell you that nobody's taking her away. She's not going anywhere. She'll never leave your heart. That precious little girl, the one who whispered her secrets in your ear and snuggled up to you in the "big bed" is still there. She lives inside you, in your deepest memories, and she'll always be there, no matter where life takes you...or her.

And something else to remember—there's just more to love. She's bagged a son for you, for petesake. Brought him home and dropped him at your feet like a prize twelve-point buck. And it doesn't hurt a thing that he is gorgeous and kind and adoring. He and your husband do boy stuff together and giggle like third-graders. He's tall enough to change any lightbulb. He eats everything that's set before him, including the garnish. Kids and dogs love him. Your daughter loves him.

What more do you want? You get to be a new mom, except you don't have to go through the trouble of birthing and raising him.

But still, you're going to cry. You're going to watch these two vibrant, beautiful young adults say their vows and take each other's hands and turn toward each other, away from you. Come prepared with plenty of tissues and a magnifying mirror, because I guarantee, you're going to lose a contact lens in a flood of tears. Just remember, watching your daughter's dreams come true is the sweetest pain you've ever felt.

CHEAT SHEET

TOO BUSY DEBATING BETWEEN 1 CORINTHIANS AND "I CARRY YOUR HEART WITH ME" BY E.E. CUMMINGS? HERE'S YOUR CHEAT SHEET:

1. When you begin your walk down the aisle, you might be overcome by some unexpected emotion. Don't freak out about it. And don't worry about looking ugly if you're crying—trust me, you don't.

2. Try to get at least one or two personal details into the ceremony. Have your little sister read a poem, or choose a passage that has a lot of meaning for you. This is your moment.

3. Stay present. Be conscious of what it feels like as you become a wife. This is one of life's transformative events. You'll always remember it if you keep your eyes open and your mind clear.

14

PARTY ON, BRIDE

Wipe off your tears of joy, grab a glass
of bubbly, put on your dancing shoes
and get ready for a kick-ass time at
your very own wedding reception

ELIZABETH

My wedding reception pretty much rocked the house. Held on the second floor of Seattle's Pan Pacific Hotel, it took over two ballrooms, an outdoor terrace, four smaller rooms and the landing over the lobby. One small room housed a chef making custom crepes to order; another was transformed into a soft-seating lounge where we kept the music quiet so guests could chat and get away from the loudspeakers. The smaller of the two ballrooms housed our cupcakes and half the dinner tables, and the larger held the dance floor and the rest of our tables. Cute signage throughout the floor encouraged guests to explore the space, and we strategically placed the three bars to get our peeps to mill about and pass Yvonne's photo booth.

Looking back, I can see how all the little lessons I learned while planning the wedding fed into the amazing reception we had. To put it bluntly, because I hadn't been a total bitch to anyone, there wasn't anything toxic about our party.

LESSON ONE: Be polite, gracious and considerate.
- Learn to say "please," "thank you," "you're right" and "yes, Mother." Even when you don't mean it. Those are going to be some of the hardest words to utter as wedding stress starts to pile up, but never forget your manners. A smile and a heartfelt "Thanks!" can make someone's day. And never underestimate the magical properties of a single chocolate truffle.

- Handwrite thank-you notes promptly, and not just for gifts. Thank your vendors and all the people who go above and beyond for you throughout your wedding planning process.

- Offer dinner to your vendors, such as your photographer, your videographer, your wedding planner and your musicians. Most places will offer you a cheaper meal option for them.

- DO NOT FLAKE on appointments. Yes, you're the bride and it's all about you, but respect other people's time and show up to all your appointments on time and in a good mood.

- Handwrite apologies when you screw up that last rule.

Remember when I forgot to write Venita a thank-you note? Imagine how icky that would have been if I'd never apologized. Thinking about that makes my insides shrivel with awkwardness.

If that's not convincing, then put yourself in the shoes of the people who have toiled and sweated for you. If you were in their place, wouldn't you feel so much better if your clients acknowledged how much they appreciated you? A week before the wedding, Dave and I sat down and prewrote thank-you notes for all our vendors. And then we stuffed the envelopes with cash. For our incredible wedding planners, who had obsessed with us, fought for us and carried us through our stressful times, we enclosed gift cards for massages at a little boutique in Seattle.

Not to sound self-serving or anything, but I felt pretty great during my reception, knowing that I was going to brighten my professional entourage's evening with a few thoughtful notes and a wad of thank-you money. Okay, that's an understatement. I felt like the Mother Teresa of brides.

LESSON TWO: Be transparent. And not in the shallow sense—just make sure that the people you interact with know your expectations, values and goals.

- Specify to your guests whether or not they're allowed to bring extras. And be gracious when someone who wasn't invited shows up.

- Give the people working for you as much inspiration as possible. Don't force your invitation designer to guess about your taste—send examples of things you like AND things you don't like. I could have saved myself a ton of time and money if I had done that from my very first updo trial.

- Find a way to graciously tell someone when you don't like something. I am TERRIBLE at this (remember how I smiled and said I loved the hairstyle that caused me to have a snot-squirting breakdown in a parking lot?). You're not doing anyone any favors by pretending to like something that just isn't right with what you want—you must gently learn how to say, "I don't know if this is exactly what I was envisioning. Could we try something a little more like *this?*" (Then whip out the inspiration photos you have because you followed the rule above.)

- Be proactive about your wedding guests' behavior.

Let's use that last rule as an example. Dave and I knew that with over fifty of our twenty-five-year-old classmates from Pomona College attending the wedding, the alcohol consumption would be off the charts (case in point: one buddy decided it would be a good idea to do a handstand on a table in the middle of a restaurant after our night-before happy hour). We had some choices: we could wring our hands about it and stress out, but do nothing and fork over the cash for the giant alcohol bill after our wedding was over; we could grow more and more bitter at our friends and their debauched ways in the weeks leading up to the Big Day; we could spend the whole evening policing everyone, knocking wineglasses out of their hands if we thought they'd had more than three drinks; or we could force everyone to pay for their own drinks at the reception. All pretty lame, right?

Then, on a trip to Costco one night, Dave and I were hit by the same bolt of inspiration-flavored lightning. We passed a display of inexpensive cases of wine, exclaimed over how cheap they were, and then realized: what if we provided mass quantities of cheap alcohol to our friends for their consumption *before* the reception? It would be like in college, when you preloaded your drunkenness before heading out to the football game!

There's still a small part of me that can't believe I'm comparing my wedding to a tailgate party.

Anyway, a week before our wedding, Dave and I went and picked up an obscene amount of beer and wine (okay, and a teensy bit of Jägermeister) for our friends. We contacted a couple of key people who could act as ringleaders after our ceremony and got them to store the booze in the bathtubs of their hotel rooms. (I wonder what the turn-down service people thought about *that*... Oh, who am I kidding? They probably thought it was awesome.) On our wedding day, while Dave and I were having our portraits taken and the less party-happy guests were having a serene cocktail hour at the reception venue, a troupe of our old classmates shotgunned, chugged and flip-cupped their way to a state of rowdiness that would have made the *Animal House* guys proud.

Now, look: I'm not saying I was thrilled about filling bathtubs with alcohol to save money on our catering bill. But given my alternatives, I'm happy we went the route we did. And I can't pretend I didn't enjoy the lap dance my friend gave me to "I'm a Slave 4 U" by Britney Spears toward the end of the night.

The takeaway here, though, is that you should be aware of some of the, ahem, *challenges* your guests might bring with them—and find a way to deal with them that will enable you to relax and enjoy yourself at the reception. And don't be shy about recruiting a couple of your more influential peeps to be the first lemmings to leap over the cliff you've designated for them.

LESSON THREE: Stick to at least a few of the traditions. Many wedding activities, like throwing the bouquet, sound cheesy. And they are. But on your wedding day, you probably won't think so—and you might just regret opting out of at least one moment of no-holds-barred wedding-themed fun. Here are some ideas:

- Shove cake in each other's faces. The photos will be priceless.

- Go ahead—toss the bouquet. But make sure you enlist your bridesmaids ahead of time to act all excited in case the response from other ladies at your wedding is tepid. And to avoid making single people feel, well, singled out, you could do what I did and say that the bouquet toss is for ALL the ladies, single or not, and whoever catches it gets good luck.

- The garter toss? Hilarious. Especially if your groom takes it off with his teeth. We almost didn't go through with it, but when I watch the video of it and see my friend Jabez wearing my garter around his forehead like a lacy Rambo, I'm so happy we did.

- Father-daughter dance. Or mother-son or mother-daughter or father-son... you get the picture. Share a dance with one of your elders. Someone who showed you the ropes. My dad and I both detest dancing, so I didn't have a father-daughter dance...and wouldn't you know it, it's one of the things I'm a little sad about when I remember our wedding. He asked me to dance for the last twenty seconds of "Stairway to Heaven," and we have a photo of it (Yvonne, our photographer, was, like, forty-seven places at once the whole time)...and I wish we'd had a more meaningful moment together.

- Dance the Hora. First, getting tossed around on a chair is like a ride at Six Flags. Second, watching gentiles attempt to figure out what they should be doing is comedic gold.

- Toasts. I spoke, I cried, my cousin spoke, I cried, my grandfather spoke and I REALLY cried (along with everyone else in the room)...then Dave's mom spoke, I laughed, Dave's big brother spoke, I chuckled, Dave's little brother spoke, and I was practically on the floor with giggles. And then, the pièce de résistance: Dave toasted me. Me! It brought the whole room to tears (again). Here's the transcript of his speech:

Hi everyone,

I have a few things I want to say. First, I want to thank everyone who helped put this weekend together. I want to pay particular tribute to the ladies at Good Taste. You are our saviors!

Next, I want to say a special thanks to our wonderful friends, Molly and Jesse, who welcomed us into their home this summer and guided us through this process. We honestly could not ask for better friends.

And I have to say thank you one more time to our parents. You have supported us, both now and over the many years as you raised us, to become the people we are today. We cannot thank you enough and we will love you now and forever.

Before I let you all eat, drink and be merry, I want to propose a toast to my wonderful bride: [he started tearing up here, so you can imagine the chorus of sniffling that broke out to serenade the rest of his toast]

She's brilliant, she's beautiful and I love EVERY little thing about her.

You all know me as a smiley, laughy guy. Well, I owe SO much of that happiness to my wonderful Wiggs. She has a sense of silliness and fun that makes me smile from a hundred yards away.

There are so many amazing things about her, but I want to single out one: her compassion. She's always there for her friends and family and she is so quick to help those in need. When we were first together, it took me a while to adjust as she emptied her wallet to people on the street. It's hard to build a budget around that. And I'm still shocked when we go grocery shopping and there's almost nothing left for us by the time we get home because she's given so much food away to people we pass on the street. But she's taught me how to see the humanity in every single person I meet, from my taxi driver to the man holding out his hat on the corner by our building. There are so many ways she has influenced me, and I'm a better man today because she is in my life.

And, finally, I have to say there's no better feeling in life than waking up next to the woman of your dreams every morning. I'm so lucky I found her. And I can't wait for a lifetime of laughter together. So cheers to my beautiful wife!

Amazing, right? Well, *I* think it is, anyway.

Ultimately, the reason my reception was such a hit for me was because I could look back on all the planning I'd done, on the life I'd built with Dave, on the life-changing moments I'd experienced along the way...and I was proud. Part of it was manners—I hadn't poisoned the wedding water by being a brat. But most of it was managing to remind myself (or have my mother remind me) of the bigger picture, especially when things got tough.

At the very end of the night, as I was belting along to Queen's "Fat Bottomed Girls" with my eyes closed, a group of about fifty people formed a long tunnel with their arms. I was so entranced by my sing-along that I didn't even notice I was the only person dancing until Dave tapped me on my shoulder and told me to turn around. He grabbed my hand, ducked his head and together we ran through a tunnel full of the faces of our loved ones, cheering us on and pouring their best wishes out to us as we stepped into our life together as husband and wife.

I may or may not have cried that it was over in the elevator on the way up to the honeymoon suite.

But then I got, you know, distracted.

And now my mother's ears are bleeding from this very slight reference to my sex life, so I'll leave it at that.

CHEAT SHEET

ATTEMPTING TO CHOREOGRAPH AN INTERPRETIVE DANCE TO "I WILL ALWAYS LOVE YOU" INSTEAD OF FINISHING THIS CHAPTER? HERE'S YOUR CHEAT SHEET:

1. Get your groom to toast you during the reception. It's so sweet to see your guy up there, telling a roomful of people exactly what he loves about you.

2. Plan out your etiquette in advance: pre-write thank-you cards and checks to your vendors, and make sure ahead of time that everyone who helped you will feel appreciated.

3. If you can stand it, do at least one little wedding tradition. Sure, tossing the bouquet or having a cake fight is cheesy and clichéd, but on your wedding day it might just be freakin' fun.

15

OFF THE
BEATEN PATH

Wedding stuff that Emily Post never
saw coming: divorced/tricky family
situations, same-sex marriages,
elopements, mixed-religious
ceremonies, etc.

ELIZABETH

Every family has its own idiosyncrasies. In the end, you have to remain true to what you really want for yourself, deep down.

There are warring families who make the Medicis seem like the Tanners on *Full House*. Some couples deal with different religious backgrounds, divorced parents or same-sex unions. Everyone's going to have an opinion on what you do, but you're the one who will have a lifetime of memories from the occasion, so trust yourself.

Today, matrimony includes a multitude of styles, beliefs and loves. When I talk about "your" fiancé I've been referring to "him." I'll let my friend Julie take it from here, since she's a little, ahem, more qualified than me to talk about marrying a foxy lady.

WIGGS: Did your mother play a part in your wedding?

JULIE: My mom passed away before any of my sisters or I could get married. During our ceremony, we took a moment to acknowledge all those who weren't able to be there.

WIGGS: What have you learned about the meaning of a wedding, both for you and your wife, and for your loved ones?

JULIE: We had two weddings—one for our family and friends and one for us.

When we were planning our ceremony, we knew that it wouldn't "count" in any kind of legal way. So for us, it was about our community committing to us as a lifelong couple. Our vows were not only vows to each other, but vows that we'd be active in further bettering our community.

This wedding felt real—as far as we knew. We still celebrate this day as our anniversary. As the weeks and months went by, we really began to realize that there was now something physical mandating our relationship to be permanent. This made me much more accountable for our relationship. We finally realized the weight of the marriage.

WIGGS: What was unique about your wedding?

JULIE: As one of our "big three must-haves," we knew there needed to be a heavy dose of live music. We held the ceremony in a music hall that had the elements of both a rock club and a chapel. We were married on stage.

Jen came down the aisle holding a candle with her parents by her side, I followed carrying a candle of my own and my father on my arm. It was dramatic and heartwrenching and SO us.

The most important thing to us was to have a wedding that could not have been anyone else's.

WIGGS: Tell me your best wedding drama story. I KNOW you've got at least one. Please. You have to. Otherwise I'll feel like a failure and my entire book will be totally lame.

JULIE: Probably the most dramatic element of my wedding was trying to find a wedding dress. I must have tried on thirty gorgeous, white, fluffy, perfect wedding gowns. Every time, I would say, "Wow. This is beautiful, and I look great... and I feel ridiculous." From the very beginning, I had my ideal wedding dress drawn on a scrap of paper. Black and white lace corset top with a piecey, kinda rock 'n' roll skirt. Believe it or not, this dress does not exist. Just when I was ready to give up, I found it. Black lace halter top with a low back (to show off my tattoos) and an asymmetrical satin pickup skirt with a big black sash around the waist. It was classy and rock 'n' roll all at the same time. I knew it would work well with the faux-hawk hairdo I had planned. Before I even zipped it up, I knew.

WIGGS: What are the three pieces of advice you'd give a bride?

JULIE:

1. Choose the three things that are your priorities for your wedding. No one can have the perfect EVERYTHING. For us it was great music, great food and an environmentalist message.
2. Delegate. If something isn't going as planned, mention it to one of your helpers and then let her take care of it.
3. Don't let your marriage just be a self-congratulatory event. Figure out what your love was put on the earth to do. Know that your marriage needs to have a purpose (and not just to stave off loneliness).

WIGGS: What resources did you find most valuable in planning your wedding? Were there any unique challenges that you and your wife faced as a same-sex couple?

JULIE: My favorite guides were the books that had some kind of punk element to them. *Anti Bride Guide: Tying the Knot Outside of the Box* was a particularly good find.

We didn't have any relatives who made a statement with their absence, or who sent nasty responses to our invitations. I bought the engagement rings outside of Dallas, and made a point of saying I was about to propose to my *girlfriend*—and they barely batted an eye.

We even had one of the girls at David's Bridal blush bright red when we told her we wanted to look at bridesmaid's dresses for our wedding. At first we thought she couldn't handle the idea—turns out she was about to propose to her girlfriend that night.

Maybe your nontraditional situation isn't being a same-sex couple.

Maybe you and your betrothed belong to different religions. Aubrey had a rabbi and a priest stand at the altar as she got married, leading her and her fiancé through various religious traditions. I was a bridesmaid and I nearly fainted (literally, and had to get another bridesmaid to prop me up) from the emotion evoked by drawing from two different spiritual cultures.

Maybe you have divorced and remarried parents, so your family has doubled in size. Susie's stepfather became "Dad" while her biological father remained "Daddy." Dad led her halfway down the aisle, where Daddy waited to escort her the rest of the way.

Maybe you don't want to have a traditional big, white wedding at all. Lindsey invited everyone to an "engagement" cocktail party. In the middle of the evening, she sneaked away and switched out of her navy blue dress and into a knee-length ivory gown and birdcage veil. Minutes later—to the delight of her guests—she appeared in the room on the arm of her father, walked to the middle of the crowd and was married to her fiancé.

You know the one thing all these couples have in common? They all say their wedding was the happiest day of their lives, and they all ended up married to their soul mates.

CHEAT SHEET

YOU MEANT TO READ THE CHAPTER, BUT THEN YOUR GRANDMA CALLED AND YOU REALIZED YOU STILL NEEDED TO TELL HER THAT YOUR WEDDING WAS GOING TO BE WICCAN? HERE'S YOUR CHEAT SHEET:

1. A wedding is a wedding is a wedding. No matter what nontraditional elements you have, you're still going to end up married at the end of it all—and that's a beautiful thing.

2. Don't let yourself get pressured into having a certain type of wedding. Map out a day that reflects the values and truths you and your fiancé hold dear.

3. Tell the nay-sayers to put a champagne cork in it. Politely.

16

THE HONEYMOON

And they lived happily ever after...

ELIZABETH

By the time Dave and I started thinking about our honeymoon, every red cent of our wedding budget was spoken for. And then some.

Early on, we'd decided not to monkey with a huge, monthlong vacation halfway across the globe. We didn't have a crystal ball, but we both knew we would be exhausted after our wedding, so we wanted to find a place to hole up and do a whole lotta nothing. Even if we'd had money left over, we wouldn't have wanted to go somewhere that would call for all-day treks to the most important tourist landmarks. And since we were broke, well...the old two-person pup tent in my parents' garage was starting to look like our only option.

"At least we won't have any wedding stuff to worry about," Dave said gingerly.

"Yeah..." I said, my skin already tingling with phantom itches in anticipation of the clouds of mosquitoes that tend to find me whenever I'm in the wilderness.

I thought back wistfully to my mom's suggestion, days into our engagement, that we honeymoon at the Château Frontenac in Quebec. Oh, well. We could have a lavish vacation some other time, when we hadn't just spent twenty grand in one day.

My mom's maternal instincts must have kicked her in the gut over this, because the day Dave and I decided to go camping for our honeymoon, she called me and asked what we were planning to do in the two weeks before we had to return to Chicago and start classes at our respective grad schools.

"Oh!" I said brightly, taking a fake-it-till-you-make-it approach to being excited about spending my first days of wedded bliss in a sleeping bag on the ground. "Well, I think we're going to go camping! You know, get away from it all, lose ourselves in the middle of nowhere..."

My mom's silence on the other line was as thick as full-fat mayonnaise.

"Yeah, and then someday we'll do a big celebratory trip, like, when we have the energy and...stuff...?" My voice trailed off.

"Well. That doesn't sound very romantic."

In my fragile, I'm-trying-to-be-okay-with-not-having-a-nice-honeymoon-even-though-my-armpit-hair-is-already-starting-to-get-furrier-in-retaliation-for-me-not-being-able-to-shave state, I got defensive. In a cantankerous tone, I lashed out at my mom.

"It's not exactly easy to have a romantic honeymoon when we don't have any money to spend on it," I snapped.

I waited for my mom's cranky reply, but instead, she said simply, "I'll call you back. I have an idea."

SUSAN

HOW THE HONEYMOON REALLY EVOLVED

In case you haven't figured it out yet, Elizabeth comes from a long line of manipulative yet goodhearted women. It seems to run in the family like a clockwise cowlick. My mother's mother was famous for convincing everyone that the only recipe she could successfully produce involved canned fruit in heavy syrup, large-curd cottage cheese and a dollop of Cool Whip, thus escaping the need to cook for years. She had more important things to do, like teaching us to play pinochle, crocheting toilet-paper covers or painting elephants on greenware mugs.

And my mother. Don't get me started. In our family, "Clara Lou" is often used as a verb. As in, "I just got Clara-Loued into leading a game of charades at the family reunion."

Elizabeth was the first grandchild, awaited by my mother with the kind of anticipation most people reserve for Halley's Comet. My daughter and my mother are as thick as thieves. I have pictures of them doing everything together, from lying in bed and taking one bite from every chocolate in the box to see what's inside, to doing each other's hair in cornrows, to knitting rugs for Barbie's dream house.

The pair of them are inseparable—and the honeymoon was no exception.

There's only one problem. Even the most evolved, easygoing and original couples are going to have a hard time bringing their grandparents along on the honeymoon.

The good news is, my mother is living proof that it can be done. And done well.

She heard through the grapevine (okay, it was me) that the wedding budget was spent, and there was little or nothing left over for a honeymoon. The bride and groom were looking into borrowing the neighbors' VW Westfalia camper, grabbing a can of mosquito repellent and heading to the Starlite Motor Court for a couple of nights. It was better than heading back to the office or lecture hall two days after the wedding, but just barely.

Grammy and Pa to the rescue! Wishing to give the happy couple a memorable gift, they decided to lavish them with a dream honeymoon. And, boy, did they.

They found a resort amid the majestic vermilion canyons of southern Utah. The Inn at Entrada has private little casitas with kitchenettes and views of the red-rock buttes and the wide western sky. It has fountains and pools, a golf course and a day spa. It has high-speed internet, endless hikes in the wilderness and HBO on Demand.

Oh, and one other thing. The dream resort, the perfect spot for the happy couple to adjust to married life *just happens to be seven miles from her grandparents' house.* Imagine that!

So Elizabeth got to have her honeymoon and her grandparents, too. Kudos to Dave for being a good sport about it all, and to the grandparents for arranging everything and for giving the newlyweds plenty of space. The bride and her grandmother did manage to organize a couple of double dates, of course.

Seriously, this is in keeping with what we all believe—that spending money on an extravagant honeymoon is one thing, but spending time with your grandparents is priceless.

ELIZABETH

Days later, Grammy called and proposed giving us a honeymoon at the resort in her town. And, Dear Readers, it was awesome. Don't ever let anyone tell you that honeymooning with your grandparents isn't fun. Dave and I had an amazing time hiking the canyons of southern Utah during the day and going out to fancy meals with Grammy and Pa each evening. Pa would order Dave a tawny port at the end of each dinner and the four of us would watch the sun go down. During these long days after my wedding, my grandparents opened up to me about their own fifty-five-year marriage, sharing the secret to staying in love forever: "Everything is fifty-fifty," Grammy told me. "No matter what."

"Yeah," said Pa, giving Dave a look that spoke volumes about another secret to a happy marriage: the wife is always right.

Sure, we didn't go to an over-water glass-floored hut in Tahiti, spending our days getting couples massages and sipping piña coladas. But—and I mean this in the mushiest way possible—I cherish the memory of our honeymoon as a time spent learning from our elders, enveloped in the love of multiple-family generations, with a little bit of prune juice thrown in to keep us regular. I wouldn't trade that for the world.

CHEAT SHEET

TOO BUSY LEARNING HOW TO SAY "MASSAGE OIL" IN FIJIAN? HERE'S YOUR CHEAT SHEET:

1. Think long and hard about how you're going to feel at the end of your wedding. I knew I would be exhausted, so I made sure my honeymoon was as undemanding as possible. If you think you'll be energized by your new-wife status, by all means, plan a backpacking trip through Iceland. But be honest with yourself.

2. Sure, the honeymoon is about you and your new spouse, but it's not the end of the world if you bump into some of your near and dear ones. If you know someone who lives near your honeymoon location, don't feel funny about visiting.

3. Honeymooning with your grandparents (or similar elders) is totally awesome. But if you don't go that far, at least sit them down sometime and bask in their wisdom.

THE BEGINNING

Final thoughts from the bride
and her mother

ELIZABETH

There was a moment toward the end of my wedding when time seemed to slow down. I looked around and saw my life's whole cast of characters: people who had watched me grow up, who had grown with me, who had stumbled their way through high school by my side, who had shaped and colored my experiences as a young woman finding her way in the world...friends and relatives, new and old, all were there because Dave and I loved each other so much we decided to throw a party about it.

I reflected on loved ones who weren't there: the college room-mate who had to take her medical exams that weekend; the aunt who doesn't travel; my feisty, auburn-haired grandmother who passed away; the childhood friend who died in a car accident when we were sixteen. I could feel them there, too, boogying down in spirit to "Walk This Way" and sending me all their love and respect.

And then there was Mommy.

See, here's the thing about your mom: she's your guardian angel. I know, sometimes it feels like she's your nemesis, like when she's disdainfully regarding the menu you've decided upon, or populating your guest list with fifty extra people two weeks before the wedding, or cutting you down mid-argument using the one tone of voice she knows you can't bear...but at the end of the day, no matter how scrappy your fights were, she's your mom.

She's the one who held your hand through life's biggest moments, from your first steps to your first day at school. She's the one who tried (unsuccessfully) to act like she wasn't devastated the day she dropped you off at college. She's the one—probably the only one—who knows every moment of your life better than you do, who has been guiding you since before you took your first breath, who has been your cheer-leader during your triumphs and your soft place to fall during your defeats.

Looking at my mom, dancing wildly with her sister at my wedding, I realized how hard this must have been for her. After today, someone else would be holding my hand and mapping my life. After today, I wasn't just her daughter. I was someone's wife.

Holy crap.

I wasn't kidding about the day she dropped me off at college—she was a train wreck. I know you probably think of my mom as this glamorous, poised novelist, but that day she was a sobbing, mascara-streaked mess. (Let's not sugarcoat this: so was I.)

I wanted to reach out to my mom right there on the dance floor and tell her I would always be her little girl. Sure, she had to share her pedestal with Dave, but there were bonds between my mother and me unlike any others. I felt like I should say something to acknowledge how wonderful, scary, exciting, difficult and enormous this day was.

At that moment, she came over and told me she was going to head home. The last ferry would be leaving soon and she needed to make sure her house-guests made it back that evening. I froze, the sappy speech I was planning stuck in my throat.

She pulled me into a fierce hug, then held me at arm's length. "I'm so proud of you, baby," she said.

"I love you, Mommy," I replied. I couldn't think of anything else to say. (Good thing I got to write a book about it so now she knows.)

And then she pointed me toward my new husband. He scooped me into his arms, twirled me around and pulled me into a mass of danc-ing friends. When I glanced at the door of the ballroom, my mom was gone.

So here I am, nearly a year later, trying to decide what to leave you with. I can already sense that the little details are fading from memory, only coming alive through Yvonne's photos or Mitch's video. Here's what will last, though: on my wedding day, I married my best friend and soul mate. Our road to the altar was giddy, joyous and, okay, sometimes a little bumpy. But through it all, guiding, judging, encouraging, snarking and cheering us on, was my mom.

Sometimes I wanted to kill her; sometimes I wanted to run to her and force her to rub my back and tell me everything would be okay. None of it mattered in the end. Mommy's love for me never faltered. She has always been and will always be my anchor.

Plus she bought me really, really, *really* great wedding shoes.

SUSAN

You did it! You made it to the end zone, over the line and you get to spike the ball. Deep, blissful sigh.

In a few weeks, the photos and video will be ready, but your part is done. Looking back you'll realize that there's no way to declare the wedding a perfect event. It did not come off like a twelve-page spread in a bridal magazine.

There will be little things. You forgot to pull on your Spanx (an oversight I heartily applaud). You forgot your earrings. And can it be... why, yes, it can. You forgot to hem your mother-of-the-bride dress. Seriously. It's there in the ultra-large-format, high-resolution photos of you dancing as if you're a legend in your own mind. The wavy-edged hem tape is hanging right there for all the world to see.

And there are other things. They'll come to you in the middle of the night, like stealthy moths, snapping you to full wakefulness: Did your last-minute heartfelt mother-daughter talk come off the way you meant it? No, it didn't. Because you didn't have The Talk with her. And that toast you gave? Lame. You cried through the whole thing. And you're supposed to be the wordsmith of the family. Oh, and you forgot to pose for pictures with relatives who traveled thousands of miles to be with you. The videographer got stuck in traffic and missed some key shots. One of the nephews sat through the entire ceremony, texting with his friends. You couldn't find your sister when R.E.M.'s "Stand" started playing. The word *hymen* was uttered over the PA system during the ceremony. It's easy to come up with a laundry list of oversights, slights and maybe even outright disasters.

News flash. The world didn't see the hem tape, or the un-spandexed hip bulge, or the lack of earrings. People loved your toast. And the mother-daughter talk? You've been doing that all her life. She knows everything you need to tell her.

Don't look back at the gaffes and regret a single moment. Take joy in what you've done. You've borne witness to one of life's greatest miracles—the start of a magnificent new love. In the words of the immortal Dr. Seuss, don't cry because it's over. Smile because it happened.

Bad moments make for good stories. And a good story, like a good marriage, lasts forever.

ACKNOWLEDGMENTS

Like a kick-ass wedding celebration, this book was a collaborative effort that never would have happened without the vision, creativity and support of a whole host of good-hearted folks.

The authors would like to thank the people at MIRA Books who conceived of the idea and made it happen—Margaret O'Neill Marbury, Deborah Brody, Adam Wilson, Donna Hayes and Loriana Sacilotto.

We are grateful to our literary agents—Meg Ruley, Annelise Robey and their colleagues at the Jane Rotrosen Agency—who offered their expertise and advice every step of the way.

The energy behind the stories we tell comes from the many thoughtful and hilarious readers of our blogs www.iamthebeholder.com and www.susanwiggs.wordpress.com.

We'd also like to extend our deepest gratitude, love and affection to our families—the in-laws, out-laws, rogues and rapscallions who made the whole journey a blast.

Last but hardly least, love and thanks to our ever-patient, good-humored and freakishly tall main character, Dave.